THE COMMUNION SERVICE

FIRST
BAPTIST
CHURCH
LIBRARY

Also by David Stone:
Your Baby's Baptism

The Communion Service

David Stone

BAPTIST CHURCH LIBRARY

Hodder & Stoughton
LONDON SYDNEY AUCKLAND

Copyright © 1996 by David Stone.

First published in Great Britain 1996.

The right of David Stone to be identified as the author of the work
has been asserted by him in accordance with the
Copyright, Designs and Patents Act 1988.

Unless otherwise indicated Scripture quotations are taken from
the HOLY BIBLE, NEW INTERNATIONAL VERSION.
Copyright © 1973, 1978, 1984 by International Bible Society.
Used by permission of Hodder and Stoughton Ltd.
All rights reserved.

Extracts from *The Book of Common Prayer*, the rights of which are
vested in the Crown, are reproduced by permission of the Crown's
Patentee, Cambridge University Press.

The Alternative Service Book 1980 is copyright © The Central Board
of Finance of the Church of England. Extracts are reproduced with
permission.

10 9 8 7 6 5 4 3 2 1

All rights reserved.
No part of this publication may be reproduced, stored in a retrieval
system, or transmitted, in any form or by any means
without the prior written permission of the publisher,
nor be otherwise circulated in any form of binding or cover
other than that in which it is published and without a similar condition
being imposed on the subsequent purchaser.

British Library Cataloguing in Publication Data
A record for this book is available from the British Library.

ISBN 0 340 64200 9

Designed and typeset by Kenneth Burnley at Typograph,
Irby, Wirral, Cheshire.
Printed and bound in Great Britain by Cox & Wyman Ltd,
Reading, Berkshire

Hodder and Stoughton Ltd
A division of Hodder Headline PLC
338 Euston Road
London NW1 3BH

✿ Contents

Acknowledgments

I'M GRATEFUL to all those who have helped during the writing of this book, in discussing the issues, supplying resource material and reading through drafts of the manuscript. My particular thanks go to Richard Barrett-Lennard, Gerald Beauchamp, Sandy Cairns, Christopher Colven, Colin Gale, Margarita Helmsing, Archbishop David Hope, David McDougall, Sandy Millar, Catheryne Mitchell, Philip Mounstephen and Rick Simpson. My thanks too to Bishop Simon Barrington-Ward for contributing a Foreword.

Scattered through the book are a number of hymns on the theme of Holy Communion, some old, some new. With the older hymns, I've chosen, by and large, to use the more modern versions published by Jubilate Hymns in *Hymns for Today's Church*, whom I'd like to thank for kindly allowing their material to be reproduced here.

Finally, I would like to thank the congregation of St Jude's Church, Courtfield Gardens, London, to whom this book is dedicated, for their partnership in the good news of Jesus Christ as we have explored and celebrated his love for us in the special meal of Holy Communion.

David Stone
October 1995

Foreword

by the Bishop of Coventry

IN ALL OUR LIVES there come times, times of deep feeling or even of numbness, times of inexpressible joy or sorrow, when simple actions mean more than any words could. A handclasp, a hug, someone offering you a place to sit down or making you a cup of tea, convey what cannot be said.

I remember a German friend telling me how, as a prisoner of war, he had felt completely alone, since he had argued against Hitler with his fellow prisoners and thus been fiercely rejected. He went for a solitary walk out at night in the camp. Suddenly, as he neared the perimeter fence, a figure on the other side of the wire moved. There was a clink of metal and some object seemed to be pointed towards him. He feared it was a weapon until a kindly English voice said, ''Ave a drop o' this, Mate!' He reached out and it was a hot billy can full of tea. 'I never drank anything that tasted so sweet', he told me. For him the action of that British sentry brought the assurance that there was still love in the world, and that nothing can break it totally or separate us from it. In spite of himself he was drawn back in again, into the family of humankind.

That surely is a parable of what the sacrament of Holy Communion has often meant to me and, I am sure, to many others. It can give us an actual physical assurance of God's love for us. Even on occasions when the word, powerfully uttered, has moved us in the course of a service, we can than find that the sign or symbol of Holy Communion, just like the actions of Jesus himself in the stories in the Gospels, really clinches the promise and fulfils the assurance of that word. The bread and wine received, truly nourish us, body and soul. As a Lutheran pastor said once to me, 'Having *heard* the word we must stay to *taste* him!'

But Holy Communion can only come to mean so much more than words alone when we have been well taught, through words, something of what it really means. The more we can be helped to understand this wonderful symbolic action of Jesus by which he continues to communicate himself to us, the more he will begin, through that communion, to make us one with him in his death and risen life.

In our churches at present, participation in Holy Communion has become more frequently and more widely the heart of our main weekly act of worship than it has ever been since earlier Christian times. But many of those who come have forgotten, if they ever knew, much of its real significance. We need to be helped to learn how to prepare ourselves, how to enter into the central action, and what it is that we are thereby receiving.

That is where this book comes in. David Stone has supplied us here with a summary of his own excellent teaching, given in his church in London. He has drawn up such a clear, comprehensive and biblical exposition of the meaning of this sacrament, that I believe many people may be helped through using what he has written. They will find together an ever fuller and richer awareness of all that God's grace has provided for us in the breaking of bread and the sharing of the cup. This book offers its readers a simple practical invitation to the Feast.

David himself, having explored all the dimensions of the sacrament, past, present and future, comes near the end of his book to the way in which Jesus gave this 'supper' to us as an enactment and a foretaste of one of his own favourite ways of portraying the kingdom itself, namely a party or a banquet to which we are summoned.

John Wesley saw in this image of the feast the very heart of the gospel of the divine love into which he sought to bring all humanity; especially the poorest, the most vulnerable, the furthest away, those on the very edge of society itself. As an old man the famous evangelist, we are told,[1] was expounding the parable of the Great Supper (Luke 14:15–24). He came to the point at which the servants returned from the highways and byways from which they had gathered in the poor, the maimed, the blind and the lame. 'And the servant said, Lord what thou dost command is done, and yet there is room.' Here the aged Wesley's self-control cracked as an eyewitness tells us: 'He lifted up his hands and, with tears flowing down his cheeks, repeated the words with great feeling, "and yet there is room; and yet there is room!"'

Through David Stone's firm, practical account of Holy Communion, may his readers be so grasped afresh by the wonder of God's gracious love for us in Christ, that they may be enabled to draw many into the fullness of his heavenly banquet.

✠ *Simon Coventry*
October 1995

🌿 Introduction

ALL OVER THE WORLD, sharing a meal together is one of the central ways in which people today express the bonds they have with one another. From formal dinners with everyone dressed in their best, to casual suppers where friends just turn up as they are, eating brings us together in a special way and helps us to build up and enjoy our relationships with one another.

This isn't simply a modern idea, though. Indeed, the sharing of a meal in biblical times was an even more significant means of bringing people together than it is now. And as well as being a social occasion, sharing a meal also had religious overtones. The practice of 'saying grace', of giving thanks to God, both before and after the meal, had a much higher profile in biblical times than it does today.

It's hardly surprising then that a shared meal has such a special part to play in the life of the Christian Church. Ever since Jesus introduced it on the night before he died, the meal of Holy Communion has had a central place in Christian worship. Different Christians call it by different names – the Breaking of Bread, the Lord's Supper, the Eucharist, the Mass, the Lord's Table – but, with very few exceptions, all agree on its vital importance (not that they necessarily agree on much else concerning it!). Perhaps it's because it *is* so significant that disputes about Holy Communion lie at the root of many of the historic divisions within the Christian Church that still exist today. It's far beyond the scope of this book to try to heal the scars that have marred the life of the Church for many centuries; instead, my intention is to suggest an

approach to Holy Communion that is primarily practical. Even
those who have grown up within the Church don't necessarily
understand all that is going on and why in Holy Communion, and
for outsiders and those new to the Christian faith, it can all seem
very confusing and obscure. Therefore the aim of this book is to
explain the background to Holy Communion, and to suggest various ways of entering more fully into what happens.

Down the years, Christians have looked to the Bible as their
ultimate source of authority when deciding what to believe and
how to behave, so I've chosen to focus mainly on what the Bible
itself says about Holy Communion. That's not to say that there is
no place for learning from how other Christians have tackled these
questions in the past, but it's important first to get the biblical
foundations sorted out before going on to the different contributions from church history.

An important point to make is that there's much more to
Holy Communion than just an hour or so on Sunday morning.
Like all Christian worship, what happens in church is simply a
reflection of life during the rest of the week. Holy Communion
doesn't take place in an isolated bubble: it's very closely related to
everything else that happens in the lives of those who take part.
This is often underlined in the prayer books of the different
churches. Here, for example, is how the Church of England's
Alternative Service Book 1980 begins its section on Holy Communion: 'Careful devotional preparation before the service is rec-
ommended for every communicant'.

It's all too easy to get so used to Holy Communion that we
take it for granted. However, we miss out on a great deal if we
approach it too casually, and it's here that this book is intended to
help as we investigate what the meal of Holy Communion means
from several different angles: Christians look *together* with believers down through the years and right across the world. They look
back to the events that the meal of Holy Communion commemo-
rates. They look *within* to identify things that are wrong with their
lives in order to put them right. They look *up* to worship and to
be at one with their living Lord. They look *around* in fellowship

with one another. They look *forward* to the wonderful future that this meal promises. And they look *out* in order to begin making a difference in a needy world.

CHAPTER 1

🌸 Looking together
The breadth of Holy Communion

IMAGINE IT'S NEARLY 11.00 a.m. on a Sunday morning and we're on our way to join a congregation in a service of Holy Communion. As we go through the door, we find . . .

Here, I'd like to be able to describe a 'typical' service of Holy Communion, but the problem is that there's no such thing. Right from the word go, there's a tremendous diversity in the way various Christians conduct this central act of worship. Just about anything that *can* be done differently probably *is* being done differently! Even in traditional Anglican (Church of England) churches, with a long history of worship being firmly based on a common prayer book, modern developments have led to many variations on the basic pattern of the Holy Communion service. (This is a trend that seems likely to continue. Prior to the publication in the year 2000 of a successor to the *Alternative Service Book 1980*, the Church of England published in 1995 a commended version of *Patterns of Worship*, a rich compendium of resource material for worship which is nothing if not diverse!)

Unity in diversity

Many Christian communities meet in church buildings, both old and new, that have been specially designed for worship. But others, following an increasing trend in recent years, meet in secular settings such as school halls or people's homes – just as, incidentally, the first Christians did (see, for example, Romans 16:5). Some services are very formal: elaborate ceremonies and rituals, special clothes worn by those taking the service, the music dominated by the church organ, and people following a precise order of service in which they know exactly what is going to happen and when. Other gatherings are more informal, with everyone wearing their ordinary clothes, using modern styles of music, and being much more laid back about exactly how the meeting proceeds. Both approaches have their advantages and their drawbacks. For example, it's good to be able to relax into the rhythm of the well-loved and familiar, and traditional approaches to worship emphasise the distinctiveness of worship and the continuity that Christians have with past generations of believers. However, familiarity with what goes on in church can sometimes lead to worship becoming routine and listless instead of bringing about a life-changing encounter with the living God. Also, traditional and archaic language can give the impression that Christianity is all about the past, as well as being very difficult for newcomers to understand. On the other hand, while modern styles of music and language emphasise the relevance of Christian faith and make worship much more accessible, they can sometimes lack depth and feel rather unsatisfying.

But despite the variety that's on offer, there *are* some common features that will usually be found, in one form or another, whenever Christians meet together to celebrate Holy Communion. It's these universal features that we will concentrate on in this book.

At the beginning

As we shall see, references in the New Testament to what actually went on in biblical times in the equivalent of our services of Holy Communion are tantalisingly brief. In fact, the earliest detailed accounts we have of how the early Christians went about celebrating Holy Communion are found in the second-century writings of a man called Justin. (He's usually known as Justin Martyr because of the manner of his death in AD 165.) Born in Samaria, Justin became a Christian in about AD 130, and some twenty years later, while in Rome, he wrote what we know as his *First Apology*. It's not that he needed to say sorry for anything, but he wanted to defend fellow Christians against rumours circulating at the time about their worship. Based on wild distortions of what went on in

Holy Communion, the opponents of Christians were accusing them of cannibalism and the drinking of blood.

The parallels between what went on in Justin's time during Holy Communion and what takes place in churches today are striking. Here's part of what he wrote:

> . . . on the day called Sunday an assembly is held in one place of all who live in town or country, and the records of the prophets or the writings of the apostles are read as time allows. Then, when the reader has finished, the president in a discourse admonishes and exhorts us to imitate these good things. Then we all stand up together and send up prayers; and as we said before, when we have finished praying, bread and wine and water are brought up, and the president likewise sends up prayers and thanksgivings to the best of his ability, and the people assent, saying the Amen; and the elements over which thanks have been given are distributed, and everyone partakes; and they are sent through the deacons to those who are not present. And the wealthy who so desire give what they wish, as each chooses; and what is collected is deposited with the president. He helps orphans and widows, and those who through sickness or any other cause are in need, and those in prison, and strangers sojourning among us; in a word he takes care of all those who are in need . . .
>
> (Justin Martyr, *The First Apology*)[1]

Meeting together on Sunday; listening to readings from the Bible and hearing them explained; offering prayers and thanksgivings; each person partaking of the bread and wine for which thanks have been given; collecting money for the needy: these are the things that Justin stresses. Each one of these features is present in today's worship too – features that those taking part have in common not only with other Christians throughout the world today, but also with Christians throughout history, going right back to the earliest days of the Church.

CHAPTER 2

❧ Looking back

Holy Communion in history

JOINING TOGETHER in Holy Communion vividly brings home to us the reality of some highly significant events from the past, for whenever Christians today celebrate Holy Communion, they are drawn back into the drama of the meal Jesus had with his twelve special followers (the disciples) on the night before his death. Each of the four Gospels in the New Testament focuses in some way on this event, often called the 'Last Supper', which comes shortly before the accounts of Jesus' arrest and trial.

How it all began

Mark's Gospel is thought by most scholars to be the earliest of the four to be written. Here's how he records the preparations:

> 12On the first day of the Feast of Unleavened Bread, when it was customary to sacrifice the Passover lamb, Jesus' disciples asked him, 'Where do you want us to go and make preparations for you to eat the Passover?' 13So he sent two of his disciples, telling them, 'Go into the city, and a man carrying a jar of water will meet you. Follow him. 14Say to the owner of the house he enters, "The Teacher asks: Where is my guest room, where I may eat the Passover with my disciples?" 15He will show you a large upper room, furnished and ready. Make preparations for us there.' 16The disciples left, went into the city and found things just as Jesus had told them. So they prepared the Passover.
>
> (Mark 14:12–16)

Passover

Notice that the Last Supper took place at Passover time, a fact that the New Testament writers see as particularly significant. The reason is that the Passover meal was then (and, for Jews today, still is) a glorious celebration of what God did in the time of Moses and Aaron, hundreds of years earlier, to rescue his people from a life of forced labour as slaves in Egypt.

Despite a whole series of miraculous interventions, the Egyptian leader Pharaoh persistently refused to allow Moses to lead the Israelites back into their own country. The final straw came one horrifying night when the Egyptians discovered that God's demand to 'let my people go' was no laughing matter. Let the Old Testament book of Exodus take up the story as God tells Moses what the people are to do:

3'Tell the whole community of Israel that on the tenth day of this month each man is to take a lamb for his family, one for each household . . .

6'Take care of them until the fourteenth day of the month, when all the people of the community of Israel must slaughter them at twilight. 7Then they are to take some of the blood and put it on the sides and tops of the door-frames of the houses where they eat the lambs. 8That same night they are to eat the meat roasted over the fire, along with bitter herbs, and bread made without yeast . . .

11'This is how you are to eat it: with your cloak tucked into your belt, your sandals on your feet and your staff in your hand. Eat it in haste; it is the LORD's Passover. 12On that same night I will pass through Egypt and strike down every firstborn – both men and animals – and I will bring judgment on all the gods of Egypt. I am the LORD. 13The blood will be a sign for you on the houses where you are; and when I see the blood, I will pass over you. No destructive plague will touch you when I strike Egypt. 14This is a day you are to commemorate; for the generations to come you shall celebrate it as a festival to the LORD – a lasting ordinance.'

(Exodus 12:3, 6–8, 11–14)

Later in the chapter, this accent on repeating the celebration year by year is emphasised:

24'Obey these instructions as a lasting ordinance for you and your descendants. 25When you enter the land that the LORD will give you as he promised, observe this ceremony. 26And when your children ask you, "What does this ceremony mean to you?" 27then tell them, "It is the Passover sacrifice to the LORD, who passed over the houses of the Israelites in Egypt and spared our homes when he struck down the Egyptians."' Then the people bowed down and worshipped.

(Exodus 12:24–7)

More than anything, the Passover is a time to look back and remember with gratitude what God did in the past to rescue his people from Egypt. Without this celebration each year, succeeding generations might become careless and forget the circumstances in which their ancestors were saved from slavery. Passover helps bring these events home so that they continue to inform and refresh the way God's people think about him. It's like a railway track whose purpose is to keep the train of faith on the right lines.

The meal of Holy Communion has a very similar purpose, though the events it celebrates are even more significant. Passover is a celebration of what God did through Moses to rescue the people of Israel from slavery in Egypt. Christians see Holy Communion as a celebration of what God has done in Jesus Christ to rescue all of humanity from the slavery of sin and death. Holy Communion is, if you like, the Christian equivalent of the Jewish Passover. In the New Testament, this is what lies behind a comment made by the apostle Paul in his first letter to the Christians at Corinth: 'For Christ, our Passover lamb, has been sacrificed . . .' (1 Corinthians 5:7).

It's as if God's deliverance of the people from Egypt was a sort of preview of the even greater deliverance that Jesus would bring about – not from slavery to Egypt, but from slavery to everything that holds us back from being the people God intends us to be. This is what lies behind the description of Jesus as 'the Lamb of God, who takes away the sin of the world!' near the beginning of John's Gospel (John 1:29). Peter's first letter picks up the same theme: 'For you know that it was not with perishable things such as silver or gold that you were redeemed from the empty way of life handed down to you from your forefathers, but with the precious blood of Christ, a lamb without blemish or defect. He was chosen before the creation of the world, but was revealed in these last times for your sake' (1 Peter 1:18–19).

* * *

Here is love, vast as the ocean,
lovingkindness as the flood,
when the Prince of life, our ransom
shed for us his precious blood.
Who his love will not remember?
Who can cease to sing his praise?
He can never be forgotten
throughout heaven's eternal days.

On the Mount of Crucifixion
fountains opened deep and wide;
through the floodgates of God's mercy
flowed a vast and gracious tide.
Grace and love, like mighty rivers,
poured incessant from above,
and heaven's peace and perfect justice
kissed a guilty world in love.

Let me all thy love accepting,
love thee, ever all my days;
let me seek thy kingdom only,
and my life be to thy praise;
thou alone shall be my glory,
nothing in the world I see;
thou hast cleansed and sanctified me,
thou thyself hast set me free.

In thy truth thou dost direct me
by thy Spirit through thy Word;
and thy grace my need is meeting,
as I trust in thee, my Lord.
All thy fulness thou art pouring
in thy love and power in me,
without measure, full and boundless
as I yield myself to thee.

(Robert Lowry)

*   *   *

The Last Supper

What is sometimes referred to as the 'institution' of Holy Communion is related by Matthew, Mark and Luke in their Gospels, and by Paul in his first letter to the Corinthians. It's interesting to note that John's Gospel does not describe it as such, for reasons we shall think about later.

The accounts we have underline the fact that Christians celebrate Holy Communion primarily because this is something that Jesus told his followers to do. The Church of England's *Book of Common Prayer* describes Holy Communion as a 'sacrament', which it goes on to define in the Catechism as 'an outward and visible sign of an inward and spiritual grace given unto us, *ordained by Christ himself*, as a means whereby we receive the same, and a pledge to assure us thereof' (my italics). The early Christians didn't think Holy Communion up for themselves: it came from Jesus himself.

Here's Mark's account of what happened on that final evening before Jesus' death:

> 22While they were eating, Jesus took bread, gave thanks and broke it, and gave it to his disciples, saying, 'Take it; this is my body.' 23Then he took the cup, gave thanks and offered it to them, and they all drank from it. 24'This is my blood of the covenant, which is poured out for many,' he said to them. 25'I tell you the truth, I will not drink again of the fruit of the vine until that day when I drink it anew in the kingdom of God.' 26When they had sung a hymn, they went out to the Mount of Olives.
>
> (Mark 14:22–6)

The account in Matthew's Gospel is very similar, and most scholars agree that the writer has simply made some minor revisions to the version in Mark. These probably reflect the slight variations to the basic formula used by different churches in their worship:

> 26While they were eating, Jesus took bread, gave thanks and broke it, and gave it to his disciples, saying, 'Take and eat; this is my body.' 27Then he took the cup, gave thanks and offered it to them, saying, 'Drink from it, all of you. 28This is my blood of the covenant, which is poured out for many for the forgiveness of sins. 29I tell you, I will not drink of this fruit of the vine from now on until that day when I drink it anew with you in my Father's kingdom.' 30When they had sung a hymn, they went out to the Mount of Olives.
>
> (Matthew 26:26–30)

Luke's account is slightly different. He seems to begin a little earlier and includes some of the other features of the Passover meal, including an earlier shared cup, which the other Gospel writers omit:

14When the hour came, Jesus and his apostles reclined at the table. 15And he said to them, 'I have eagerly desired to eat this Passover with you before I suffer. 16For I tell you, I will not eat it again until it finds fulfilment in the kingdom of God.' 17After taking the cup, he gave thanks and said, 'Take this and divide it among you. 18For I tell you I will not drink again of the fruit of the vine until the kingdom of God comes.' 19And he took bread, gave thanks and broke it, and gave it to them, saying, 'This is my body given for you; do this in remembrance of me.' 20In the same way, after the supper he took the cup, saying, 'This cup is the new covenant in my blood, which is poured out for you. 21But the hand of him who is going to betray me is with mine on the table. 22The Son of Man will go as it has been decreed, but woe to that man who betrays him.'

(Luke 22:14–22)

Paul's first letter to the Corinthians, which was probably written even earlier than the Gospels, shows one form in which these instructions were passed on in the early years of the Church:

23For I received from the Lord what I also passed on to you: The Lord Jesus, on the night he was betrayed, took bread, 24and when he had given thanks, he broke it and said, 'This is my body, which is for you; do this in remembrance of me.' 25In the same way, after supper he took the cup, saying, 'This cup is the new covenant in my blood; do this, whenever you drink it, in remembrance of me.'

(1 Corinthians 11:23–5)

The emphasis in all these passages is that of *remembering* Jesus, as Christians look back on his death and its significance for them. We think back to the events of the first Holy Week (the week leading up to Easter Sunday) and the way they point forward to what was about to happen on Good Friday.

The new covenant

Notice the use of the word 'covenant' in the passages quoted above. From ancient times, the relationship between God and his people has been expressed in a series of special agreements called 'covenants'. There are parallels here with the treaties made between victorious kings and those they conquered, in which promises of protection were offered in exchange for obligations of obedience and loyalty.

The history of the Old Testament is a history of the covenants between God and his people being broken. It's all very well them promising to obey God – but the problem is that they can't! The Old Testament prophets saw that the inherent weakness of humanity makes it impossible for people to keep their side of the bargain. The answer to this is something foretold by the prophet Jeremiah – a 'new' covenant:

> 31'The time is coming,' declares the LORD, 'when I will make a new covenant with the house of Israel and with the house of Judah. 32It will not be like the covenant I made with their forefathers when I took them by the hand to lead them out of Egypt, because they broke my covenant, though I was a husband to them,' declares the LORD. 33'This is the covenant that I will make with the house of Israel after that time,' declares the LORD. 'I will put my law in their minds and write it on their hearts. I will be their God, and they will be my people. 34No longer will a man teach his neighbour, or a man his brother, saying, "Know the LORD," because they will all know me, from the least of them to the greatest,' declares the LORD. 'For I will forgive their wickedness and will remember their sins no more.'
>
> (Jeremiah 31:31–4)

Christians believe that the death of Jesus marked the sealing of this new covenant between God and humanity and that this was anticipated by Jesus in what he said at the Last Supper: 'This cup is the new covenant in my blood . . .' The apostle Paul picks up this concept of something new ('the law of the Spirit of life') to replace the old ('the law of sin and death') in his letter to the Romans:

> [1]Therefore, there is now no condemnation for those who are in Christ Jesus, [2]because through Christ Jesus the law of the Spirit of life set me free from the law of sin and death. [3]For what the law was powerless to do in that it was weakened by the sinful nature, God did by sending his own Son in the likeness of sinful man to be a sin offering. And so he condemned sin in sinful man, [4]in order that the righteous requirements of the law might be fully met in us, who do not live according to the sinful nature but according to the Spirit.
>
> (Romans 8:1–4)

Remember, remember . . .

Whoever is conducting the Holy Communion service re-enacts what Jesus did during the Last Supper, following the four-fold action described in the New Testament accounts of taking the bread and the wine, offering thanks to God, breaking the bread, and then giving the elements to the members of the congregation. Those taking part are encouraged to let their minds dwell on the way in which Jesus gave up his life in selfless love. He allowed himself not only to die, which would have been amazing enough, but to be tortured to death by crucifixion for those he came to save.

*   *   *

Christ Jesus,
being in very nature God,
did not consider equality with God something to be held onto,
but made himself nothing,
taking the very nature of a servant,
being made in human likeness.
And being found in appearance as a man,
he humbled himself
and became obedient to death –
even death on a cross!

(based on Philippians 2:5–8)

This stimulus to remember is a central part of the service. Some Christians recite what Paul writes in 1 Corinthians 11. Others use versions of what are often very ancient prayers of consecration that have been handed down from past generations. Here, for example, is a translation of one of the earliest patterns for such a prayer. It's from the *Apostolic Tradition* of St Hippolytus, thought by most scholars to date from early in the third century:

Bishop: The Lord be with you.
People: And with your spirit.
Bishop: Let us lift up our hearts.
People: We lift them up to the Lord.
Bishop: Let us give thanks to the Lord.
People: It is right and proper.
Bishop: We give thanks to you, O God, through your beloved Child Jesus Christ whom you have sent us in these last days as Saviour, Redeemer and Messenger of your plan; who is your inseparable Word, through whom you have created all things; and whom, in your good pleasure, you have sent down from heaven into the womb of a virgin; and who, having been conceived, became incarnate and was shown to be your son, born of the Holy Spirit and the Virgin; who fulfilling your will and acquiring for you a holy people, stretched out his hands as he suffered to free from suffering those who trust in you; who, when he was handed over to voluntary suffering, in order to destroy death and to break the chains of the devil, to tread down hell beneath his feet, to bring out the righteous into light, to set the term and to manifest the resurrection, taking bread, gave thanks to you and said, Take, eat; this is my Body which is broken for you; likewise the cup, saying, This is my Blood which is shed for you. When you do this, do it in memory of me. Mindful, therefore, of his death and resurrection, we offer you this bread and this cup, giving thanks to you for accounting us worthy to stand before you and to minister to you as priests.

And we ask you to send your Holy Spirit upon the offering of holy Church. In gathering [them] together grant to all those who share in your holy [mysteries] [so to partake] that they may be filled with the Holy Spirit for the strengthening of their faith in truth; in order that we may praise you and glorify you through your Child Jesus Christ, through whom be to you glory and honour with the Holy Spirit in holy Church now and throughout all ages. Amen.

(Peter G. Cobb, *The Study of Liturgy*)[1]

It's worth noting that Hippolytus is careful to stress that this isn't a fixed form that must always be used. Instead, it's set out for church leaders to use simply as a model for their own prayers. The latter is the approach followed by some Christian traditions in our own day, as leaders and/or members of the congregation are invited to lead prayers in their own words. Other churches are rather more cautious about allowing such freedom, and prescribe the precise form of words to be used. But whether using a fixed order of service or spontaneous prayers, all Christians agree on the need to look back and remember these past events and their significance, so that they continue to shape the way we think about God and his love.

This is a vitally important part of the Christian life. For example, having a Christian faith has many advantages, but it carries no guarantee that bad things will not happen to us from time to time. In facing such suffering and hardship, Christians can sometimes be tempted to think that God has forgotten about them and no longer cares. This is where Holy Communion can be such a great help. It focuses on the greatest display of God's love, reminds us of the tremendous investment that he has made in us, and gives us tangible assurance that he most certainly does still care! In chapter 8 of his letter to the Romans, Paul puts it like this:

[31] . . . If God is for us, who can be against us? [32]He who did not spare his own Son, but gave him up for us all – how will he not also, along with him, graciously give us all things?

33Who will bring any charge against those whom God has chosen? It is God who justifies. 34Who is he that condemns? Christ Jesus, who died – more than that, who was raised to life – is at the right hand of God and is also interceding for us. 35Who shall separate us from the love of Christ? Shall trouble or hardship or persecution or famine or nakedness or danger or sword? 36As it is written: 'For your sake we face death all day long; we are considered as sheep to be slaughtered.' 37No, in all these things we are more than conquerors through him who loved us. 38For I am convinced that neither death nor life, neither angels nor demons, neither the present nor the future, nor any powers, 39neither height nor depth, nor anything else in all creation, will be able to separate us from the love of God that is in Christ Jesus our Lord.

(Romans 8:31–9)

So, as Paul writes a little further on in his first letter to the Corinthians, 'For whenever you eat this bread and drink this cup, you proclaim the Lord's death until he comes' (1 Corinthians 11:26). With most of the great heroes of the past, the thing we want to focus on is their life – but this is not the case with Jesus. His life was certainly pretty extraordinary, to put it mildly, but he told his followers to remember his *death*. Above everything else, this is what Christians look back to in the meal of Holy Communion.

*   *   *

Here, O my Lord, I see you face to face,
here faith can touch and handle things unseen;
here I will grasp with firmer hand your grace
and all my weariness upon you lean.

Here I will feed upon the bread of God,
here drink with you the royal wine of heaven;
here I will lay aside each earthly load,
here taste afresh the calm of sin forgiven.

I have no help but yours, nor do I need
another arm but yours to lean upon;
it is enough, my Lord, enough indeed,
my hope is in your strength, your strength alone.

Mine is the sin, but yours the righteousness;
mine is the guilt, but yours the cleansing blood:
here is my robe, my refuge, and my peace;
your blood, your righteousness, O Lord my God.

Too soon we rise, the symbols disappear;
the feast, though not the love, is past and done:
gone are the bread and wine, but you are here,
nearer than ever, still my shield and sun.

Feast after feast thus comes and passes by,
yet, passing, points to that glad fast above;
giving sweet foretaste of the festal joy,
the Lamb's great bridal feast of bliss and love.

(Horatius Bonar)[2]

CHAPTER 3

🌸 Looking within

Dealing with the inner nature

ONE OF THE THINGS Jews do just before Passover time is to search out and get rid of all traces of yeast in the house. What's wrong with yeast? The answer is that, in the Bible, yeast is a symbol of evil – perhaps because of the way it swells up and bubbles! Anyway, whatever the reason, yeast represents the things in people's lives that must be rooted out and thrown away.

Inner spring cleaning!

This is something that carries over into Holy Communion as well. Here's the conclusion Paul draws from the parallel between the Jewish Passover and its Christian equivalent: 'For Christ, our Passover lamb, has been sacrificed. Therefore let us keep the Festival, not with the old yeast, the yeast of malice and wickedness, but with bread without yeast, the bread of sincerity and truth' (1 Corinthians 5:7–8).

For the Jews, the process of going through the house looking for yeast could be called an acted-out parable. In other words, the point isn't that God is allergic to yeast, but that he is dead set against the evil that it symbolises. The time leading up to Holy Communion is therefore a particularly appropriate opportunity for Christians to reflect on their lives and deal with anything that falls short of God's standards.

This is why services of Holy Communion usually include prayers of penitence for the confession of sin: to help worshippers to clear away any 'yeast of evil' that may be contaminating their lives. In many churches, this beautiful Collect for Purity, which probably dates from the eighth century, sets the tone near the beginning of the service (a collect is a special prayer, usually said by the presiding minister, which is intended to gather together or 'collect' the individual prayers of the congregation):

Almighty God,
to whom all hearts are open,
all desires known,
and from whom no secrets are hidden:
cleanse the thoughts of our hearts
by the inspiration of your Holy Spirit,
that we may perfectly love you,
and worthily magnify your holy name;
through Christ our Lord. Amen.

This 'looking within' is vitally important, for Holy Communion is no ordinary meal that Christians share together. This is special. So special, in fact, that Paul writes this about it:

27. . .whoever eats the bread or drinks the cup of the Lord in an unworthy manner will be guilty of sinning against the body and blood of the Lord. 28A man ought to examine himself before he eats of the bread or drinks of the cup. 29For anyone who eats and drinks without recognising the body of the Lord eats and drinks judgment on himself. 30That is why many among you are weak and sick, and a number of you have fallen asleep. 31But if we judged ourselves, we would not come under judgment. 32When we are judged by the Lord, we are being disciplined so that we will not be condemned with the world.

(1 Corinthians 11:27–32)

These are solemn words. In biblical imagery, 'falling asleep' refers to the bleak stillness of the dead rather than the peaceful slumber of the living! Paul wants his readers to grasp the fact that those who participate in Holy Communion must be worthy of it. This aspect really seized popular imagination during the Middle Ages, when ordinary Christian people dared not receive the bread and wine without the sort of rigorous preparation that most of them could only undertake once a year during the season of Lent (the few weeks leading up to Easter). For many people, this was the only occasion in the year when they would play a full part in the service rather than just watch from the sidelines.

By contrast, many churches today celebrate Holy Communion at least weekly, often as the main Sunday service. This brings with it the danger of becoming over-familiar and casual in worship, and perhaps there's a case for recapturing something of the awe and wonder with which our medieval ancestors approached Holy Communion. Taking more care in preparation is one way of ensuring that this special celebration is taken more seriously. In fact, there are a number of ways of doing this, some of which we will look at in Chapter 4.

Forgiveness

Tabloid newspapers rather enjoy revelling in people's wrongdoings, sin, but the Bible explores the subject from a rather different angle. First, what the Bible says about the characters it describes shows how *sin spoils people's lives*. Of course, one of the problems is that this isn't always evident at the time. Sins may be 'naughty' but, at least in the short term, they often do feel very 'nice'. Therefore when faced with questions of right and wrong, people often want to say, 'It feels so good – how can it possibly be doing any harm?' People sometimes think that God is a sort of celestial kill-joy, who immediately makes up a commandment to forbid anything he sees us enjoying. Nothing could be further from the truth. His commands are for our own good. To break them may not seem to do much harm at the time, but in the end it's bound to lead into the worst sort of slavery there is: slavery to selfish desires and all the damage this can do to people and their relationships.

And it's not just us. For, secondly, the Bible makes a link between human sin and everything else that goes wrong in the world. It tells us that *sin spreads*. Human beings are so intertwined with the world around us that our sin acts like a crack that runs through the whole of creation. Right at the beginning of the Bible, the consequences of the first sin affect not only Adam and Eve, but also the world around them. Here's what God tells Adam:

> [17]. . . Because you listened to your wife and ate from the tree about which I commanded you, 'You must not eat of it,' cursed is the ground because of you; through painful toil you will eat of it all the days of your life. [18]It will produce thorns and thistles for you, and you will eat the plants of the field. [19]By the sweat of your brow you will eat your food until you return to the ground, since from it you were taken; for dust you are and to dust you will return.
>
> (Genesis 3:17–19)

In the New Testament, Paul brings this aspect out in his letter to the Romans:

> [19]The creation waits in eager expectation for the sons of God to be revealed. [20]For the creation was subjected to frustration, not by its own choice, but by the will of the one who subjected it, in hope [21]that the creation itself will be liberated from its bondage to decay and brought into the glorious freedom of the children of God. [22]We know that the whole creation has been groaning as in the pains of childbirth right up to the present time.
>
> (Romans 8:19–22)

Thirdly, the Bible concludes that *sin separates people from God*. Here's a passage from the Old Testament book of the prophet Isaiah in which he responds to the charge that God has given up answering his people's prayers: 'Surely the arm of the LORD is not too short to save, nor his ear too dull to hear. But your iniquities have separated you from your God; your sins have hidden his face from you, so that he will not hear' (Isaiah 59:1–2). A sin is anything that falls short of God's ideal for human life. Some sins are big, others are small, but all of them matter. Like a single ink blot on a clean sheet of paper, just one sin is enough to contaminate our lives and so cut us off from God. Sin simply cannot survive in the presence of the white-hot purity of his nature. That's why there is a barrier between people and God; that's why he so often seems to be unreal.

Now when it comes to Holy Communion, it's not that those who take part have to be perfect and entirely without sin. As we're reminded elsewhere in the New Testament, 'If we claim to be without sin, we deceive ourselves and the truth is not in us' (1 John 1:8). The point is that all sin must be confessed and forgiven sin.

The wonderful thing that this meal teaches us is that all sin *can* be forgiven sin! The Bible puts it like this: '. . . if we confess our sins, he is faithful and just and will forgive us our sins and purify us from all unrighteousness' (1 John 1:9). This is what prevents penitence (or this 'looking inwards') from being an entirely depressing and gloomy experience. Such introspection would be morbid and unhealthy if it did not have such a positive outcome. Self-examination may be a bit of a tunnel, yes, but the light at the end is wonderful!

But how can it be 'right' to forgive sins like this? Once again, here are the words of Jesus: 'This is my blood of the covenant, which is poured out for many for the forgiveness of sins' (Matthew 26:28). This is just one of the instances where Jesus points to the fact that his death results in forgiveness and freedom for those who put their trust in him. That's why, as we saw earlier, his death is to be remembered in this way.

The Baptist Union's *Patterns and Prayers for Christian Worship* includes this encouragement to those who feel unworthy as they contemplate taking Holy Communion:

Come to this table,
not because you must
but because you may,
not because you are strong
but because you are weak.

Come, not because of any goodness of your own gives you
   the right to come,
but because you need mercy and help.
Come, because you love the Lord a little
and would like to love him more.
Come, because he loved you and gave himself for you.
Come and meet the risen Christ,
for we are his body.

(William Barclay, *The Lord's Supper*)[1]

There's a similar emphasis in the Church of England's Holy
Communion service, both in the traditional *Book of Common
Prayer* and in what is called Rite B of the *Alternative Service Book
1980*. Here, worshippers are helped to realise that, despite the fact
that they have fallen short of God's standards, Holy Communion
is indeed for them:

Hear what comfortable words our Saviour Christ saith
unto all that truly turn to him.

Come unto me all that travail and are heavy laden,
and I will refresh you. (Matthew 11:28)

So God loved the world, that he gave his
   only-begotten Son,
to the end that all that believe in him should not perish,
but have everlasting life. (John 3:16)

Hear also what Saint Paul saith.
This is a true saying, and worthy of all men to be received,
that Christ Jesus came into the world to save
   sinners. (1 Timothy 1:15)

Hear also what Saint John saith.
If any man sin, we have an advocate with the Father,
Jesus Christ the righteous;
and he is the propitiation for our sins. (1 John 2:1)

(from the Church of England's *Book of Common Prayer*)

We have the assurance of Jesus himself that our sins can be forgiven. After all, this is why he came into the world in the first place. As the angel told Joseph when he first became aware of Mary's pregnancy and was thinking of breaking off their engagement: '. . . Joseph son of David, do not be afraid to take Mary home as your wife, because what is conceived in her is from the Holy Spirit. She will give birth to a son, and you are to give him the name Jesus, because he will save his people from their sins' (Matthew 1:20–21).

Mark's Gospel underlines the same truth. He reports an occasion when Jesus' followers are arguing about which of them is the greatest. Jesus reprimands them and adds this: 'For even the Son of Man did not come to be served, but to serve, and to give his life as a ransom for many' (Mark 10:45).

Luke's Gospel has the same emphasis. The reaction of John the Baptist's father Zechariah, following John's birth, is a case in point. Filled with the Holy Spirit, Zechariah speaks out about John in words that have become known as the *Benedictus*:

> 76And you, my child, will be called a prophet of the Most High; for you will go on before the Lord to prepare the way for him, 77to give his people the knowledge of salvation through the forgiveness of their sins, 78because of the tender mercy of our God, by which the rising sun will come to us from heaven 79to shine on those living in darkness and in the shadow of death, to guide our feet into the path of peace.
>
> (Luke 1:76–9)

This forgiveness of sins is the very thing Christians meet to celebrate in Holy Communion, and this good news of release and freedom is one of the central features of the Christian message. The answer to sin is not to try and pretend that it doesn't really exist, and just to hope that it will somehow go away by itself. There's no need for people to try and hide their sins and pretend they're better than they are. That would be rather like having a cleaner come and tidy up the house on Wednesday, but then spending the whole of Tuesday running round trying to clear the place up in preparation!

Those who take such a look within may do so with a degree of shame, yes, but not with despair. God has seen it all before: he cannot be shocked. There is no stain of the soul that is beyond his power to shift if it is brought to him in repentance (turning away from it to the best of our ability) and faith (trusting in his power to save and deliver).

Individuals need to be specific at this point, bringing to mind the particular sins that are on their consciences. As a gathered congregation, Christians often join together in a formal prayer of confession of sin, either as a prayer that they all say together or as a series of responses. The Church of England uses this as one of the optional prayers at this point:

> Father eternal, giver of light and grace,
> we have sinned against you and against our neighbour,
> in what we have thought,
> in what we have said and done,
> through ignorance, through weakness,
> through our own deliberate fault.
> We have wounded your love,
> and marred your image in us.
> We are sorry and ashamed,
> and repent of all our sins.
> For the sake of your Son Jesus Christ, who died for us,
> forgive us all that is past;
> and lead us out from darkness
> to walk as children of light. Amen.
>
> (One of the confessions from the Church of England's
> *Alternative Service Book 1980*)

*   *   *

Come and see, come and see
Come and see the King of love;
see the purple robe and crown of thorns he wears.
Soldiers mock, rulers sneer
as he lifts the cruel cross;
lone and friendless now, he climbs towards the hill.

We worship at your feet,
where wrath and mercy meet,
and a guilty world is washed by love's pure stream.
For us he was made sin –
oh, help me take it in.
Deep wounds of love cry out 'Father, forgive.'
I worship, I worship the Lamb who was slain.

Come and weep, come and mourn
for your sin that pierced him there;
so much deeper than the wounds of thorn and nail.
All our pride, all our greed,
all our fallenness and shame;
and the Lord has laid the punishment on him.

Man of heaven, born to earth
to restore us to your heaven.
Here we bow in awe beneath your searching eyes,
from your tears comes our joy,
from your death our life shall spring;
by your resurrection power we shall rise.

(Graham Kendrick)[2]

*   *   *

Facing up to failure

In thinking about sin and guilt, it's important to notice the
difference between 'sin' and 'sins'. Sins are the wrong things people do, think or say – such as breaking the Ten Commandments,
for example, which are sometimes read out during a formal ser-

vice of Holy Communion. To break any of these Commandments is to commit a sin. But *sin* (singular with, if you like, a capital 'S') is the attitude of self-centredness from which such *sins* (plural, with a small 's') spring. Sin is when people put themselves at the centre of their lives, the place where God rightfully belongs. Sin is rebellion, hostility, pride, refusal to believe, showing contempt for God. It is the inner attitude that deforms and distorts people so that they become turned in on themselves instead of being opened up to God and to other people as he intends them to be.

How do we respond to this? One reaction is to say, 'Well, hold on a minute, I may not be perfect, but I'm no worse than anyone else.' That may well be true, but it doesn't let us off the hook. God is perfectly well aware that sin is a universal problem, that 'all have sinned and fall short of the glory of God' (Romans 3:23). However, God still considers us guilty. And as James reminds us, 'For whoever keeps the whole law and yet stumbles at one point is guilty of breaking all of it' (James 2:10). That's because sin is not primarily about actions, but about the *attitude* of self-centred rebellion that is at their root.

A second reaction might be this: 'OK, I know I am a sinner, but it's not my fault. I can't help it. It would be unjust of God to hold me guilty.' But God *does* hold us responsible. Sin is not simply a disease from which people need to be cured or a slavery from which they need to be set free. It is certainly like these things in some ways, but it is not *only* that. The fact that people are fallen and weak human beings may diminish their responsibility, but it does not do away with it altogether.

A number of years ago I had a car that had, without my realising it, developed a bald tyre. This was noticed by a passing policeman, and in due course the case came to court. Now, being unskilled in such things, I had left the mechanical side of my car to the care of a friend. Since he hadn't said anything about the tyres, I assumed that all was well. I tried to explain this to the court, but although they were able to sympathise with my careless choice of friends, the responsibility, though admittedly diminished through ignorance, was still basically mine. And so the fine came out of *my* bank account, not my friend's; and it was *my* licence that was endorsed, not his.

Of course there is a sense in which people are at the mercy of their genes, their background and upbringing – and the advice (or lack of it!) of their friends. It's true that, as people grow older, they can be trapped by habit into finding it more difficult to choose what is right. Ultimately, though, people use their weakness as an excuse for not resisting temptation more than they do. Freedom may be limited, but it has not disappeared altogether. People *are* responsible for their sin, and to deny this fact is to deny the freedom of choice that is an essential part of what being a human being is about.

All of us have sinned, and all of us are responsible. That makes us guilty, deserving of punishment. The Bible urges us to face the fact that we are the objects of God's holy wrath and righteous anger, and the result of sin is death, the complete separation from God for ever that we now experience in part. And that's not because God is spiteful or malicious; it simply reflects the fact that the darkness of self-centred rebellion cannot survive in the light of his presence. So our greatest need is to be forgiven, to be put in the right, to have our 'debts paid' – and we cannot do that ourselves.

But hold on a minute. There's a third response we might make. If God is as loving as he is supposed to be, why all this talk about his anger and punishment? Why can't God simply forgive us? After all, he told us to forgive our enemies – why doesn't he just do the same?

If you were to tread on my toes, it would be fairly easy for me to forgive you. It wouldn't cost me very much. But suppose that you stole £10 from me and went out and spent it all on a slap-up feast at your local McDonald's – for me to forgive you then would not be quite so easy. It would cost me something to put things right – the £10 I no longer have.

That's how it is with sin. It isn't something that a holy and just God *can* simply brush under the carpet of heaven. There's a price to be paid before guilt can be taken away. What Christians celebrate in Holy Communion is the simple truth that the price *has* been paid. The way *has* been made open for us to be forgiven and, to use the biblical word for it, 'justified' – put in the right with God. Sin need no longer be held against us. The answer to guilt lies in the cross of Jesus Christ, in people understanding what was going on as he died and in accepting for themselves what he achieved on the cross on our behalf. This is why, in church, a prayer of confession of sin is followed by the minister giving an *absolution* (an assurance of forgiveness), like this one from the Scottish Episcopal Church:

> God who is both power and love,
> forgive you and free you from your sins,
> heal and strengthen you by his Spirit,
> and raise you to new life in Christ our Lord. Amen.[3]

Going on to take part in Holy Communion – eating the bread and drinking the wine – is the outward counterpart of the inner spiritual reality of receiving the benefits of Christ's death, of accepting the truth that sins *can be* forgiven and *are* forgiven. While he was Archbishop of Canterbury in the sixteenth century, Thomas Cranmer began the process that eventually led to the publication of the Church of England's *Book of Common Prayer*. Here's how he put it: 'Our Saviour Christ, knowing us to be in this world, as it were, but babes and weaklings in faith, hath ordained sensible signs and tokens, whereby to allure and draw us to more strength and more constant faith in him . . .'[4] Just as we know our physical bodies are being fed by the bread and wine, so we trust that our souls are being fed by the broken body and poured-out blood of Christ. This isn't something that we can actually *see* happening, of course, but the bread and the wine act as visual aids to help us to grasp more fully the inner meaning of what we are doing.

Outwardly, the death of Jesus by crucifixion at the age of only 33 was a tragic end to a promising career, but the New Testament does not let it rest there. Jesus' death was not some ghastly accident that happened by mistake while God's back was turned. In fact, the whole point of Jesus' life was his death. Here's how Peter puts it: 'He himself bore our sins in his body on the tree, so that we might die to sins and live for righteousness; by his wounds you have been healed' (1 Peter 2:24). At the heart of the Christian faith lies this great exchange: Jesus' righteousness and purity for my sin and guilt; his riches in exchange for my rags.

How do people take this on board for themselves? The simple answer is that they have to decide that they want to. That is to say, we must make the decision that we really do want to turn our back on our self-centred rebellion, be forgiven for the past, and to be given the power to live new and increasingly God-centred lives in the future. We decide, in other words, that we want to be *real* Christians (Christ-ones) instead, perhaps, of just calling ourselves such. And then, trusting what Jesus has done on our behalf, we ask God for it. In New Testament terms, we repent and we believe. We take our rags, the rags of self-centred rebellion, and hand them over to Jesus so that he can clothe us in his righteousness, the righteousness of a life centred on him and his standards.

> Most merciful Lord,
> your love compels us to come in.
> Our hands were unclean,
> our hearts were unprepared;
> we were not fit
> even to eat the crumbs from under your table.
> But you, Lord, are the God of our salvation,
> and share your bread with sinners.
> So cleanse and feed us
> with the precious body and blood of your Son,
> that he may live in us and we in him;
> and that we, with the whole company of Christ,
> may sit and eat in your kingdom. Amen.
>
> (The 'Prayer of Humble Access' from
> the Church of England's *Alternative Service Book 1980*)

True and false guilt

Is that then the end of guilt? Is that all there is to it? Well no, not quite. We have looked at guilt from God's perspective and seen it as an objective reality that can be done away with. But, especially when people come to examine their lives in preparation for Holy Communion, it's important to look at guilt from the human perspective as well. It's at this point that we need to make a distinction between *feeling* bad and actually *being* bad. Guilt as a subjective feeling need not necessarily have much to do with guilt as an objective fact. As well as actually *being* guilty, people sometimes *feel* guilty as well. These two often match up: we feel guilty because we *are* guilty. However, these two things don't *always* match up: in other words, sometimes we don't always feel as guilty as we actually are, or we aren't always actually as guilty as we feel.

It's rather like having an ulcer. Imagine first that there is an ulcer in your stomach. Try and visualise what it might look like. But now, secondly, imagine (or perhaps remember from past experience!) the painful symptoms of an ulcer. There's an important difference between these two stages. There are some ulcers that are free of symptoms, and so go unnoticed and untreated. Yet there are others that have accompanying painful symptoms, and so can be successfully treated. And, just to complicate things further, there are some pains that, though they mimic the symptoms of an ulcer, are actually due to something else.

The idea that we are guilty can come from one of three different sources and it's important to sort out which is which.

The first source of this guilt is from God himself. God, by his Holy Spirit, convicts us of things in our lives that are wrong – just as Jesus said he would (John 16:8–11). That is to say, he puts his finger on areas in our lives that are not running according to his plan, and he implants a sense of unease until we confess and deal with whatever it happens to be.

However, not all senses of inner unease are from God. A second source is from the devil (Satan), the great spiritual enemy of our souls. He loves to spoil our relationship with God and to destroy the sense of peace we have. Therefore, the devil's strategy is to accuse us (Revelation 12:10), to tempt us into thinking that we are outside the scope of God's grace, and that what we've done simply can't be forgiven.

And if that wasn't enough, there's a third route for guilt mentioned in the Bible: the way in which we tend to condemn ourselves. Some people find it more difficult to forgive themselves than God does; and so, just as my small niece Hannah needs help in unwrapping her birthday presents, such people may sometimes need help in accepting God's pardon and peace. Some churches include a formal prayer of absolution in which the minister declares the truth that God promises to forgive those who turn to him in repentance and faith, but sometimes even this is not enough. Therefore one of the important tasks and privileges of the Christian minister is to help people apply these biblical truths about sin and forgiveness to themselves personally. Some church traditions stress this more than others and some require their members to take part in such confession regularly. But whatever your own background, if you need help in receiving the forgiveness the Bible speaks of, then do seek out help.

How can we distinguish between the convicting voice of God and the condemning voices of the devil and our own hearts? Let me suggest this. God is always *specific*: he puts his finger on things that are wrong and clearly directs us to the source of forgiveness. Yet that's the last thing the devil wants, and his accusations are often much more general and ill-defined. Instead of a finger he uses a sledge-hammer. His strategy is to try and persuade us that the wrong things we're conscious of lie completely outside God's ability to forgive. We need to face the devil's lies with the truth: the rock-solid guarantee of our full forgiveness is the death of Jesus Christ on our behalf. There is no sin so great that it cannot be cleansed by his blood: 'Let us then approach the throne of grace with confidence, so that we may receive mercy and find grace to help us in our time of need' (Hebrews 4:16). This is what we celebrate as, in Holy Communion, we look within ourselves.

Love

Love bade me welcome: yet my soul drew back,
  Guiltie of dust and sinne.
But quick-ey'd Love, observing me grow slack
  From my first entrance in,
Drew nearer to me, sweetly questioning,
  If I lack'd any thing.

A guest, I answer'd, worthy to be here:
  Love said, You shall be he.
I the unkinde, ungratefull? Ah my deare,
  I cannot look on thee.
Love took my hand, and smiling did reply,
  Who made the eyes but I?

Truth Lord, but I have marr'd them: let my shame
  Go where it doth deserve.
And know you not, sayes Love, who bore the blame?
  My deare, then I will serve.
You must sit downe, sayes Love, and taste my meat:
  So I did sit and eat.

                        (George Herbert, *The Temple*, 1633)

CHAPTER 4

Taking a closer look within
The process of self-examination

> *I weave a silence on to my lips,*
> *I weave a silence into my mind,*
> *I weave a silence within my heart.*
> *I close my ears to distractions,*
> *I close my eyes to attractions,*
> *I close my heart to temptations.*
> *Calm me, O Lord, as you stilled the storm,*
> *Still me, O Lord, keep me from harm,*
> *Let all the tumult within me cease,*
> *Enfold me, Lord, in your peace.*

(David Adam)[1]

* * *

WE SAW in the last chapter that Holy Communion needs to include looking within ourselves. But how are people to go about examining themselves and identifying the 'yeast of evil' that needs to be done away with? First, this is something that needs time and concentration, and this is one of the reasons why it's a good idea to arrive some minutes before a Holy Communion service is due to start. Taking time to prepare in this way is a vital investment for what lies ahead. Some people also find it helpful to go without food (called fasting) before coming to church. Fasting seems to be less widely practised these days, but it can really help people to focus more closely on their spiritual lives rather than being distracted by their physical needs and desires. It's mentioned in the context of prayer several times in the Bible (for example, 1 Samuel 7:6; Isaiah 58:3–12; Matthew 6:16–18; Acts 13:1–2).

Helping Christians in this process of self-examination is an important aspect of the work of the Holy Spirit, and planting in us a sense of unease about the way we fall short of God's standards is something we can expect him to do. Although the Holy Spirit sometimes does this directly, his usual method is to draw our attention to a relevant verse or story in the Bible. As the Bible itself says, the word of God is the 'sword of the Spirit' (Ephesians 6:17); and the writer to the Hebrews affirms that '. . . the word of God is living and active. Sharper than any double-edged sword, it penetrates even to dividing soul and spirit, joints and marrow; it judges the thoughts and attitudes of the heart' (Hebrews 4:12).

This is one of the reasons why we pay so much attention to the Bible in our services of Holy Communion, with direct readings from it and sermons or talks intended to explain its meaning and apply its truths to our lives. Indeed, in the Church of England, Holy Communion is the only service at which a sermon *must* be preached. Even though a sermon is often included in other services of worship, it's an optional ingredient. A service of Holy Communion is intended to reflect a balance of word and sacrament in the spiritual diet of the Christian.

However, a balanced spiritual diet needs to include not only this public teaching based on the Bible, but also individual prayer and meditation on the Scriptures in private. A good habit to get into is that of reading a passage of the Bible each day and then pausing to reflect on it prayerfully. If you're not used to this (or even if you are!), you will find there are a number of different publications to help you with such Bible study.[2] These publications suggest appropriately 'bite-sized portions' of the Bible to read each day, and offer guidance in the form of questions and brief comments.

One purpose of such a daily exercise is to help us to draw on the help of the Holy Spirit in our own lives. For the Bible doesn't only help us to get to know *God* better; it also helps us to get to know *ourselves* better. The longest of the Psalms focuses especially on this function of the word of God. Here are the first two sections:

> 1Blessed are they whose ways are blameless,
>   who walk according to the law of the LORD.
> 2Blessed are they who keep his statutes and seek him
>   with all their heart.
> 3They do nothing wrong; they walk in his ways.
> 4You have laid down precepts that are to be fully
>   obeyed.
> 5Oh, that my ways were steadfast in obeying your
>   decrees!
> 6Then I would not be put to shame when I consider
>   all your commands.
> 7I will praise you with an upright heart as I learn your
>   righteous laws.
> 8I will obey your decrees; do not utterly forsake me.
> 9How can a young man keep his way pure? By living
>   according to your word.
> 10I seek you with all my heart; do not let me stray from
>   your commands.
> 11I have hidden your word in my heart that I might not
>   sin against you.
> 12Praise be to you, O LORD; teach me your decrees.
> 13With my lips I recount all the laws that come from
>   your mouth.
> 14I rejoice in following your statutes as one rejoices in
>   great riches.
> 15I meditate on your precepts and consider your ways.
> 16I delight in your decrees; I will not neglect your
>   word.
>
> (Psalm 119:1–16)

In the New Testament, James writes about the 'word of God' being like a mirror in which we see ourselves reflected. This is a picture that underlines the need for action – the whole point of the illustration is that we don't look at ourselves in a mirror simply as an end in itself (or at least we shouldn't!), but with the aim of identifying and putting right anything that we find to be wrong:

> 21Therefore, get rid of all moral filth and the evil that is so prevalent, and humbly accept the word planted in you, which can save you. 22Do not merely listen to the word, and so deceive yourselves. Do what it says. 23Anyone who listens to the word but does not do what it says is like a man who looks at his face in a mirror 24and, after looking at himself, goes away and immediately forgets what he looks like. 25But the man who looks intently into the perfect law that gives freedom, and continues to do this, not forgetting what he has heard, but doing it – he will be blessed in what he does.
>
> (James 1:21–5)

Such self-examination should be a part of the day-to-day spiritual lives of Christians as they reflect on the Bible. Yet from time to time, we may feel that it's appropriate to examine our lives even more closely and systematically. So in the remainder of this chapter, we'll look at a number of different ways of facing up specifically to the challenging standards of God's word as laid out in the Bible.

God's Law – the Ten Commandments

Some churches' orders of service include an opportunity for the reading of the Ten Commandments or the summary of God's Law declared by Jesus and recorded in each of the first three Gospels.

Here are the Ten Commandments as set out in the Old Testament book of Exodus:

> 1. I am the LORD your God, who brought you out of Egypt, out of the land of slavery. You shall have no other gods before me.

2. You shall not make for yourself an idol in the form of anything in heaven above or on the earth beneath or in the waters below. You shall not bow down to them or worship them; for I, the LORD your God, am a jealous God, punishing the children for the sin of the fathers to the third and fourth generation of those who hate me, but showing love to a thousand generations of those who love me and keep my commandments.

3. You shall not misuse the name of the LORD your God, for the LORD will not hold anyone guiltless who misuses his name.

4. Remember the Sabbath day by keeping it holy. Six days you shall labour and do all your work, but the seventh day is a Sabbath to the LORD your God. On it you shall not do any work, neither you, nor your son or daughter, nor your manservant or maidservant, nor your animals, nor the alien within your gates. For in six days the LORD made the heavens and the earth, the sea, and all that is in them, but he rested on the seventh day. Therefore the LORD blessed the Sabbath day and made it holy.

5. Honour your father and your mother, so that you may live long in the land the LORD your God is giving you.

6. You shall not murder.

7. You shall not commit adultery.

8. You shall not steal.

9. You shall not give false testimony against your neighbour.

10. You shall not covet your neighbour's house. You shall not covet your neighbour's wife, or his manservant or maidservant, his ox or donkey, or anything that belongs to your neighbour.

(Exodus 20:2–17)

Notice that the Ten Commandments deal first with our relationship with God, and then move on to deal with our relationships with one another. Here's a summary of what each one is getting at:

1. Make sure that God always comes first in your life.
2. Don't let your worship focus on outward things in place of God himself.
3. Don't misuse God's name or swear.
4. Don't misuse God's day.
5. Love and respect your family.
6. Don't let your anger get out of control.
7. Don't misuse sex.
8. Don't steal.
9. Don't lie or distort the truth.
10. Don't envy others, but be content with what you have.

God's law – the perspective of Jesus

Matthew's Gospel includes the following account of how Jesus replied when asked which one was the most important of the Ten Commandments. Notice that he refused to narrow it down to just one – the absolute basic minimum is two!

> [34]Hearing that Jesus had silenced the Sadducees, the Pharisees got together. [35]One of them, an expert in the law, tested him with this question: [36]'Teacher, which is the greatest commandment in the Law?' [37]Jesus replied: '"Love the Lord your God with all your heart and with all your soul and with all your mind." [38]This is the first and greatest commandment. [39]And the second is like it: "Love your neighbour as yourself." [40]All the Law and the Prophets hang on these two commandments.'
>
> (Matthew 22:34–40)

Jesus is getting at the fact that obedience to God's Law is a matter of right *attitudes* rather than just right *actions*. To try and deal with sin as though it were just a matter of what we do and say is like trying to clear a garden by simply chopping down the undesirable weeds. This is fine for a while, but if the roots are still in place it's inevitable that the weeds will soon return.

This is what Jesus deals with in what we call the Sermon

on the Mount. In his day, some people seemed to have got it into their heads that keeping God's Law was simply about what you did, and that what you were really like on the inside wasn't that important. Here's Jesus' robust response to this attitude:

20For I tell you that unless your righteousness surpasses that of the Pharisees and the teachers of the law, you will certainly not enter the kingdom of heaven. 21You have heard that it was said to the people long ago, 'Do not murder, and anyone who murders will be subject to judgment.' 22But I tell you that anyone who is angry with his brother will be subject to judgment. Again, anyone who says to his brother, 'Raca,' is answerable to the Sanhedrin. But anyone who says, 'You fool!' will be in danger of the fire of hell. 23Therefore, if you are offering your gift at the altar and there remember that your brother has something against you, 24leave your gift there in front of the altar. First go and be reconciled to your brother; then come and offer your gift. 25Settle matters quickly with your adversary who is taking you to court. Do it while you are still with him on the way, or he may hand you over to the judge, and the judge may hand you over to the officer, and you may be thrown into prison. 26I tell you the truth, you will not get out until you have paid the last penny. 27You have heard that it was said, 'Do not commit adultery.' 28But I tell you that anyone who looks at a woman lustfully has already committed adultery with her in his heart. 29If your right eye causes you to sin, gouge it out and throw it away. It is better for you to lose one part of your body than for your whole body to be thrown into hell. 30And if your right hand causes you to sin, cut it off and throw it away. It is better for you to lose one part of your body than for your whole body to go into hell. 31It has been said, 'Anyone who divorces his wife must give her a certificate of divorce.' 32But I tell you that anyone who divorces his wife, except for marital unfaithfulness, causes her to become an adulteress, and anyone who marries the divorced woman commits adultery. 33Again, you have heard that it was said to the people long ago, 'Do not break your oath, but keep the oaths you have made to the Lord.' 34But I tell you, Do not swear at all: either by heaven, for it is God's throne; 35or by the earth, for it is his footstool; or by Jerusalem, for it is the city of the Great King. 36And do not swear by your head, for you cannot make even one hair white or black. 37Simply let your 'Yes' be 'Yes', and your 'No', 'No'; anything beyond this comes from the evil one. 38You have heard that it was said, 'Eye for eye, and tooth for tooth.' 39But I tell you, Do not resist an evil person. If someone strikes you on the right cheek, turn to him the other also. 40And if someone wants to sue you and take your tunic, let him have your cloak as well. 41If someone forces you to go one mile, go with him two miles. 42Give to the one who asks you, and do not turn away from the one who wants to borrow from you. 43You have heard that it was said, 'Love your neighbour and hate your enemy.' 44But I tell you: Love your enemies and pray for those who persecute you, 45that you may be sons of your Father in heaven. He causes his sun to rise on the evil and the good, and sends rain on the righteous and the unrighteous. 46If you love those who love you, what reward will you get? Are not even the tax collectors doing that? 47And if you greet only your brothers, what are you doing more than others? Do not even pagans do that? 48Be perfect, therefore, as your heavenly Father is perfect.

(Matthew 5:20–48)

Looking at our lives in the light of God's Law as laid out in the Bible is one way of examining ourselves, but there are also other ways of going about it. Here are a number of other passages from the Bible that can guide us. They're not designed to be used all at once – select whichever seems most appropriate for you at the time.

The fruit of the Holy Spirit

We begin with a list of contrasts that the apostle Paul sets out in his letter to the Galatians:

16So I say, live by the Spirit, and you will not gratify the desires of the sinful nature. 17For the sinful nature desires what is contrary to the Spirit, and the Spirit what is contrary to the sinful nature. They are in conflict with each other, so that you do not do what you want. 18But if you are led by the Spirit, you are not under law. 19The acts of the sinful nature are obvious: sexual immorality, impurity and debauchery; 20idolatry and witchcraft; hatred, discord, jealousy, fits of rage, selfish ambition, dissensions, factions 21and envy; drunkenness, orgies, and the like. I warn you, as I did before, that those who live like this will not inherit the kingdom of God. 22But the fruit of the Spirit is love, joy, peace, patience, kindness, goodness, faithfulness, 23gentleness and self-control. Against such things there is no law. 24Those who belong to Christ Jesus have crucified the sinful nature with its passions and desires. 25Since we live by the Spirit, let us keep in step with the Spirit.

(Galatians 5:16–25)

Paul sees the Christian life as a conflict between the new life of the Holy Spirit within believers and the old life of their sinful nature. As new Christians soon discover, becoming a Christian does not lead to the instant annihilation of the sinful nature. Temptation remains very real, and part of us continues to find sin intensely attractive. However, the difference is that, whereas beforehand we had little choice in the matter, we are now able to decide whether to 'gratify the desires of the sinful nature' (verse 16) or to 'keep in step with the Spirit' (verse 25). Paul's two lists of our sinful nature contrasted with life guided by the Holy Spirit help us to discover which way we are living. Reflect on each of the items Paul mentions. What evidence is there in your life of the 'acts of the sinful nature'? What evidence is there that your life is producing the 'fruit of the Spirit' instead? Now pray for forgiveness and ask for a fresh infusion of the Holy Spirit's power in the light of your self-examination.

True happiness

As we've already seen, the teaching of Jesus in the Sermon on the Mount is a very exacting standard against which we can examine ourselves. 'Be perfect, therefore, as your heavenly Father is perfect' (Matthew 5:48) is hardly the easiest of the Bible's commands to obey! Here's what Jesus says before the passage we examined earlier:

> 3'Blessed are the poor in spirit,
> 　for theirs is the kingdom of heaven.
> 4Blessed are those who mourn,
> 　for they will be comforted.
> 5Blessed are the meek,
> 　for they will inherit the earth.
> 6Blessed are those who hunger and thirst for righteousness,
> 　for they will be filled.
> 7Blessed are the merciful,
> 　for they will be shown mercy.
> 8Blessed are the pure in heart,
> 　for they will see God.
> 9Blessed are the peacemakers,
> 　for they will be called sons of God.
> 10Blessed are those who are persecuted because of
> 　　righteousness,
> 　for theirs is the kingdom of heaven.
> 11Blessed are you when people insult you, persecute you and falsely say all kinds of evil against you because of me. 12Rejoice and be glad, because great is your reward in heaven, for in the same way they persecuted the prophets who were before you. 13You are the salt of the earth. But if the salt loses its saltiness, how can it be made salty again? It is no longer good for anything, except to be thrown out and trampled by men. 14You are the light of the world. A city

on a hill cannot be hidden. 15Neither do people light a lamp and put it under a bowl. Instead they put it on its stand, and it gives light to everyone in the house. 16 In the same way, let your light shine before men, that they may see your good deeds and praise your Father in heaven.

(Matthew 5:3–16)

These are challenging words. Try them in reverse and see how you match up:

Sad are those who think a lot of themselves,
     for theirs is the dominion of darkness.
Sad are those who gloss over evil,
     for they will be made to face up to it.
Sad are the proud,
     for they have nothing to look forward to.
Sad are those who can't be bothered about right and wrong,
     for they will be unfulfilled.
Sad are the unforgiving,
     for they will get what they deserve.
Sad are those who are unclean on the inside,
     for they will never see God.
Sad are those who stir up trouble,
     for they will be called children of the devil.
Sad are those who give in at the first sign of trouble,
     for the kingdom of heaven is not theirs.

Using the Psalms

This is part of Psalm 139: 'Search me, O God, and know my heart; test me and know my anxious thoughts. See if there is any offensive way in me, and lead me in the way everlasting' (Psalm 139:23–4). A number of the Psalms were written to express regret and sorrow for sin, and reading these thoughtfully can help us to identify areas in our own lives that need attention. Here, for example, is Psalm 51:1–17, a Psalm that reflects the aftermath of the events described in 2 Samuel 11 and 12:

*For the director of music. A psalm of David. When the
prophet Nathan came to him after David had committed
adultery with Bathsheba.*

¹Have mercy on me, O God,
    according to your unfailing love;
  according to your great compassion
    blot out my transgressions.
²Wash away all my iniquity
    and cleanse me from my sin.
³For I know my transgressions,
    and my sin is always before me.
⁴Against you, you only, have I sinned
    and done what is evil in your sight,
  so that you are proved right when you speak
    and justified when you judge.
⁵Surely I was sinful at birth,
    sinful from the time my mother conceived me.
⁶Surely you desire truth in the inner parts;
    you teach me wisdom in the inmost place.
⁷Cleanse me with hyssop, and I shall be clean;
    wash me, and I shall be whiter than snow.
⁸Let me hear joy and gladness;
    let the bones you have crushed rejoice.
⁹Hide your face from my sins
    and blot out all my iniquity.
¹⁰Create in me a pure heart, O God,
    and renew a steadfast spirit within me.
¹¹Do not cast me from your presence
    or take your Holy Spirit from me.
¹²Restore to me the joy of your salvation
    and grant me a willing spirit, to sustain me.
¹³Then I will teach transgressors your ways,
    and sinners will turn back to you.
¹⁴Save me from bloodguilt, O God,
  the God who saves me,

and my tongue will sing of your righteousness.
15O Lord, open my lips,
     and my mouth will declare your praise.
16You do not delight in sacrifice, or I would bring it;
     you do not take pleasure in burnt offerings.
17The sacrifices of God are a broken spirit;
     a broken and contrite heart,
     O God, you will not despise.

Love

1 Corinthians 13 is one of the best-loved chapters in the Bible, but it's also one of the most challenging. Try reading it through and inserting your own name in place of the word 'love' to get some idea of those areas where your life might need to be put right. Verses 1 to 7 are given below:

1If I speak in the tongues of men and of angels, but have not love, I am only a resounding gong or a clanging cymbal. 2If I have the gift of prophecy and can fathom all mysteries and all knowledge, and if I have a faith that can move mountains, but have not love, I am nothing. 3If I give all I possess to the poor and surrender my body to the flames, but have not love, I gain nothing. 4Love is patient, love is kind. It does not envy, it does not boast, it is not proud. 5It is not rude, it is not self-seeking, it is not easily angered, it keeps no record of wrongs. 6Love does not delight in evil but rejoices with the truth. 7It always protects, always trusts, always hopes, always perseveres.

Marks of a disciple

A number of years ago, David Watson wrote a book called simply *Discipleship*3. It includes the following very challenging set of questions for Christians to ask themselves about how closely they are following Jesus. I have changed the form of the questions into the first person:

1. **Am I willing to serve?** This was a repeated lesson that Jesus had to teach his status-seeking disciples, especially when he humbled them dramatically by washing their feet (John 13; cf. Mark 10:35–45).

2. **Am I willing to listen?** When Simon Peter was full of bright ideas on the mountain where the Transfiguration took place, God told him to 'listen' to his Son (Luke 9:35). When Martha was impatiently bustling around preparing a meal while Jesus was talking, she was gently rebuked for not being like her sister Mary, who was sitting quietly listening to Jesus (Luke 10:41f.).

3. **Am I willing to learn?** When Jesus spoke about his coming sufferings and death, Peter blurted out, 'Never, Lord! This shall never happen to you.' Jesus' stinging reply was something Peter never forgot (Matthew 16:22f.).

4. **Am I willing to be corrected?** How well do I receive honest criticism, when others speak the truth in love? (Matthew 18:15).

5. **How well do I submit to the authority of those above me?** (1 Thesssalonians 5:12f.; Hebrews 13:17). Am I willing to do this, even when I do not understand all the reasons why, or when I do not naturally enjoy what I am being asked to do?

6. **Can I share my life with others, in open and honest fellowship?** (1 John 1).

7. **Am I learning humility?** Can I rejoice with those who rejoice, and be genuinely glad when others are blessed in some way or other? (Philippians 2:3f.).

8. **Am I learning to examine myself before criticising others?** (Matthew 7:1–5).

9. **Do I know my weaknesses?** Am I learning to overcome them by the grace of God? (2 Corinthians 12:9).

10. **Am I a perfectionist?** This will lead me into either self-righteousness, self-condemnation, self-pity or a judgmental spirit. 'We all make many mistakes' (James

3:2; cf. 1 John 1:8–10). Am I learning to accept myself as God accepts me in Christ – just as I am?

11. **Am I able to forgive?** (Matthew 18:21f.).

12. **Do I have 'stickability'?** Or do I give up easily? How do I handle discouragements? (Ephesians 6:10ff.; cf. 2 Corinthians 4:7ff.).

13. **Am I to be trusted?** (1 Corinthians 4:2). Am I reliable? Will I get on with a task without constant nagging? Am I willing to trust others, even when they have disappointed me and let me down?

14. **Do I mind my own affairs?** Or am I always wanting to pry into the lives of others, becoming a busybody or even a gossip? (John 21:21f.; 1 Timothy 5:13).

15. **Do I do little things well?** (Colossians 3:17).

16. **How do I use my leisure time?** Do I see that all of my time is a gift of God to be used wisely? (Ephesians 5:15–17).

17. **Do I aim first and foremost to please God?** Or do I seek the praise of others, or gratify my own desires? (John 12:43; 2 Corinthians 5:9).

18. **Am I quick to obey when God speaks to me?** When fisherman Peter instantly obeyed the instructions of Jesus on the Sea of Galilee, however foolish those instructions may have seemed to him, there were astonishing results (Luke 5:4–9). This proved a vital lesson (which had to be learned more than once!) in the years ahead.

19. **Have I faith in God, especially when there may be no outward signs to encourage my faith?** (Luke 18:1–8; Mark 11:12ff.).

20. **Where is my security?** Am I willing to trust ultimately in the love and faithfulness of God, or do I look for more temporal and material securities first and foremost? (Matthew 6:19–34). Am I willing to move as the Spirit leads me on, to make adjustments and changes, or do I resist change?

21. **Have I a clear understanding of God's priorities for my life?** (Acts 6:2–4).

*　　　*　　　*

When I survey the wondrous Cross,
on which the Prince of glory died,
my richest gain I count but loss,
and pour contempt on all my pride.

Forbid it, Lord, that I should boast
save in the death of Christ my God;
all the vain things that charm me most,
I sacrifice them to his blood.

See from his head, his hands, his feet,
sorrow and love flow mingled down;
did e'er such love and sorrow meet,
or thorns compose so rich a crown?

His dying crimson like a robe,
spreads o'er his body on the Tree;
then am I dead to all the globe,
and all the globe is dead to me.

Were the whole realm of nature mine,
that were an offering far too small;
love so amazing, so divine,
demands my soul, my life, my all!

(Isaac Watts, 1674–1748)

CHAPTER 5

❧ Looking up

Jesus in Holy Communion

WHEN CHRISTIANS gather together to celebrate Holy Communion they are not focusing on a dead hero from the past. It's not like a group of Elvis Presley fans gathering at his old home of Gracelands to remember the so-called 'King'. No: this is much more than a service of commemoration. It's a *communion* with Jesus. For Christians believe that as they gather together in communion, Jesus is actually with them to nourish and sustain them as they take the bread and the wine in remembrance of him.

A sequence of events recorded in John's Gospel helps to bring out what this actually means in practice. At the beginning of John 6, Jesus performs an amazing miracle in which 5,000 people are fed from the slenderest of resources. Just how slender they are is reflected in John's almost dismissive description of the 'five small barley loaves and two small fish'! (John 6:9). The next day, with the crowd gathering in hope of a repeat performance of this miracle, Jesus encourages them to reach beyond merely physical food. Why? Because it doesn't last, and so cannot feed that within them which is designed to last for ever: 'Do not work for food that spoils, but for food that endures to eternal life, which the Son of Man will give you . . .' (John 6:27). It turns out that by 'food that endures to eternal life', Jesus means nothing less than himself, and that the way to get such food is by believing in him: 'Then Jesus declared, "I am the bread of life. He who comes to me will never go hungry, and he who believes in me will never be thirsty"' (John 6:35). This point is emphasised again a little later as Jesus stresses: 'I tell you the truth, he who believes has everlasting life'

(John 6:47). He goes on to tell the people exactly how it is that belief in him leads to eternal life. It's clearly linked with his death, an event that will result in life for others: 'I am the living bread that came down from heaven. If anyone eats of this bread, he will live for ever. This bread is my flesh, which I will give for the life of the world' (John 6:51).

This leads his audience into some heated discussion, to which Jesus replies in very stark terms:

> [52]Then the Jews began to argue sharply among themselves, 'How can this man give us his flesh to eat?' [53]Jesus said to them, 'I tell you the truth, unless you eat the flesh of the Son of Man and drink his blood, you have no life in you. [54]Whoever eats my flesh and drinks my blood has eternal life, and I will raise him up at the last day. [55]For my flesh is real food and my blood is real drink. [56]Whoever eats my flesh and drinks my blood remains in me, and I in him. [57]Just as the living Father sent me and I live because of the Father, so the one who feeds on me will live because of me.'
> (John 6:52–7)

What Jesus says here is not *primarily* about Holy Communion at all. Certainly, at this stage in John's Gospel, his hearers wouldn't have understood him in such terms. The events of the Last Supper – the last meal Jesus took with his disciples before his crucifixion – are still a long way off. No, what matters first and foremost is that they who heard then and we who read now should *believe in Jesus*. Even when we do go on to apply this passage to Holy Communion (as the reference to blood in verse 53 suggests we should), the main emphasis is still on this inner reality of faith to which eating the bread and drinking the wine are the external counterparts. As one commentator on John's Gospel puts it: 'This section is certainly not out of place when read in the context of the Lord's Supper, provided we never lose sight of the cruciality of faith, both for coming to Christ and for the renewal of our communion with him in the feast he has instituted.'[1]

The imagery Jesus employs here is nothing if not vivid! To believe in him is like eating his flesh and drinking his blood. This is what Holy Communion is all about. 'Believe and thou hast eaten' is how St Augustine summarised it. Or, to put it less crudely, to believe in Jesus is to receive him in such a way that he is incorporated into our life and we into his. It's about remaining in him and he in us (John 6:56).

*   *   *

Bread of heaven, on you we feed,
for your flesh is food indeed;
always may our souls be fed
with this true and living bread,
day by day our strength supplied
through your life, O Christ, who died.

Vine of heaven, your precious blood
seals today our peace with God;
Lord, your wounds our healing give,
to your cross we look and live:
Jesus, with your power renew
Those who live by faith in you.

(J. Conder)[2]

*   *   *

How this translates into daily life is brought out in an incident that takes place after Jesus' resurrection and is described at the end of John 20. When Jesus first appears to his disciples, Thomas is absent:

> [25]When the other disciples told him that they had seen the Lord, he [Thomas] declared, 'Unless I see the nail marks in his hands and put my finger where the nails were, and put my hand into his side, I will not believe it.' [26]A week later his disciples were in the house again, and Thomas was with them. Though the doors were locked, Jesus came and

stood among them and said, 'Peace be with you!' 27Then he said to Thomas, 'Put your finger here; see my hands. Reach out your hand and put it into my side. Stop doubting and believe.' 28Thomas said to him, 'My Lord and my God!' 29Then Jesus told him, 'Because you have seen me, you have believed; blessed are those who have not seen and yet have believed.' 30Jesus did many other miraculous signs in the presence of his disciples, which are not recorded in this book. 31But these are written that you may believe that Jesus is the Christ, the Son of God, and that by believing you may have life in his name.

(John 20:25–31)

For Thomas, believing in Jesus means, first of all, acknowledging who he is: his Lord and his God. But it doesn't stop there; Thomas goes on to put this belief into practice by worshipping Jesus. This is what it really means to believe. As we shall see, to worship Jesus is not simply about what we do in church on Sunday: kneeling down and saying prayers or standing up and singing hymns. It's about obedience – treating him as what we acknowledge him to be: our Teacher, Master and Lord, not just on Sunday, but throughout the week.

Holy Communion is indeed a 'communion', a joining together as one, a means whereby, through faith, we share Jesus' life and he shares ours. This is what Christians celebrate in Holy Communion as they rejoice in the living presence of their risen Lord. Even though the main focus is on the events of Jesus' death, it's not an occasion for sorrow or mourning. Death met its match in Jesus Christ, as John's vision of him vividly sets out: 'Do not be afraid. I am the First and the Last. I am the Living One; I was dead, and behold I am alive for ever and ever! And I hold the keys of death and Hades' (Revelation 1:17–18).

Sunday

Rather than continuing with the Jewish custom of observing what we now call Saturday as the Sabbath day of rest and worship, the early Christians set aside Sunday, the first day of the week. Why? Because this was the day when Jesus rose from the dead. (Matthew 28:1; Mark 16:2; Luke 24:1; John 20:1). Thus it was only natural for his followers to mark the day of this triumphant victory over death by setting time aside to gather together for worship (Acts 20:7; 1 Corinthians 16:2).

What Christians throughout the world have celebrated on the first day of every week since then is that 'it was impossible for death to keep its hold on him' (Acts 2:24). Jesus slipped through death's fingers and rose from the dead, never to die again: 'After he had provided purification for sins, he sat down at the right hand of the Majesty in heaven' (Hebrews 1:3). That's why, in Holy Communion, Christians believe that they look up in worship to their *living* Lord. Indeed, this is what we mean by describing the service as a *communion*: an expression of the relationship between Jesus in heaven and his people on earth.

Such worship will sometimes be enthusiastic and exuberant. At other times there will be a sense of stillness and a deep, almost tangible, silence. In many Christian traditions, such diversity is reflected in the rhythm of the church's year and the imaginative use of language, music, posture and colour. In recent years, a wealth of material has been made available to give worship a distinct flavour at different times of the year.[3] Services tend to be more reflective and penitential in tone during the seasons of Advent, Lent and Holy Week. Thus, churches that normally say or sing the Gloria (see page 86) and Alleluias tend not to do so for these periods of the church year. ('Alleluia', or 'Hallelujah', comes from the Hebrew for 'Praise the Lord!', often found in the Psalms and in depictions of the worship of heaven in Revelation 19.) By contrast, the accent is more on expressing joy and celebration (the more Alleluias the better!) at Christmas, Easter and Pentecost. But whatever the style of worship, at its heart lies the life-changing encounter between worshippers and their Lord.

*   *   *

Thanks be to you,
Lord Jesus Christ,
for all the pains and insults you took in my place:
for all the many blessings you have won for me.
Most merciful Redeemer, Friend and Brother,
may I know you more clearly,
love you more dearly,
and follow you more nearly,
day by day. Amen.

(A prayer by St Richard, Bishop of Chichester,
in the thirteenth century)

*   *   *

Stooping to conquer

We noticed in Chapter 2 that John's Gospel doesn't include an account of the institution of Holy Communion. If, as most scholars think, John's was the final one of the four Gospels to be written, it may simply be that he didn't feel the need to duplicate what the others had already set out. There are hints elsewhere in John's Gospel about the meaning and significance of Holy Communion – especially, as saw earlier, in John 6 – but there's nothing at all where we would expect it (somewhere around John 13). Instead, we have this account of Jesus washing his disciples' feet:

> [1]It was just before the Passover Feast. Jesus knew that the time had come for him to leave this world and go to the Father. Having loved his own who were in the world, he now showed them the full extent of his love. [2]The evening meal was being served, and the devil had already prompted Judas Iscariot, son of Simon, to betray Jesus. [3]Jesus knew that the Father had put all things under his power, and that he had come from God and was returning to God; [4]so he got up from the meal, took off his outer clothing, and wrapped a towel around his waist. [5]After that, he poured water into a basin and began to wash his disciples' feet, dry-

ing them with the towel that was wrapped around him. 6He came to Simon Peter, who said to him, 'Lord, are you going to wash my feet?' 7Jesus replied, 'You do not realise now what I am doing, but later you will understand.' 8'No,' said Peter, 'you shall never wash my feet.' Jesus answered, 'Unless I wash you, you have no part with me.' 9'Then, Lord,' Simon Peter replied, 'not just my feet but my hands and my head as well!' 10Jesus answered, 'A person who has had a bath needs only to wash his feet; his whole body is clean. And you are clean, though not every one of you.' 11For he knew who was going to betray him, and that was why he said not every one was clean. 12When he had finished washing their feet, he put on his clothes and returned to his place. 'Do you understand what I have done for you?' he asked them. 13'You call me "Teacher" and "Lord", and rightly so, for that is what I am. 14Now that I, your Lord and Teacher, have washed your feet, you also should wash one another's feet. 15I have set you an example that you should do as I have done for you. 16I tell you the truth, no servant is greater than his master, nor is a messenger greater than the one who sent him. 17Now that you know these things, you will be blessed if you do them.'

(John 13:1–17)

Of course we can't be certain why John chooses to include this story instead of an account of the institution of Holy Communion. However, one suggestion is that by the time John was writing his Gospel, there may well have been those in the Church who had got so used to Holy Communion that they were beginning to take it for granted, and eating the bread and drinking the wine without really thinking about what they mean. And so perhaps John writes in order to correct the attitude of those who assumed that simply to come along and eat the bread and drink the wine would automatically do them good. This may be why, instead of following the example of the other Gospel writers and describing the events of the Last Supper in detail, John puts in something else instead. Thus in order to prevent his readers from being distracted by the signs of bread and wine themselves, John leaves them out altogether. What we are left with is a powerful summary of the underlying meaning of the Last Supper.

First of all, this incident sets out to underline the most important thing about Holy Communion: the way it demonstrates the extent of Jesus' love. After all, how do we really know that Jesus loves us? And how much does he love us? It's not so much what Jesus *says* that answers this question with such clarity and power, but what he *does*. Verse 1 says: 'Having loved his own who were in the world, he now showed them the full extent of his love.' What follows is an extraordinary picture. The Lord of all heaven and earth kneels in front of each of his disciples in turn, including even Judas Iscariot, the traitor who is shortly to betray him. One by one, he washes and dries their feet. In this graphic and unmistakable way, Jesus shows his disciples the lengths he is prepared to go for them, how far he is prepared to stoop to conquer for them. For this is a task that only the lowliest slave would have undertaken. This is how Jesus demonstrates his willingness to go on even further. The one who washes the disciples' feet is the one who is also prepared, in just a few hours, to endure for them the humiliation and degradation of death by hanging on a cross. And it's not just for the disciples. It's as if John's readers too are seated round that same table. Jesus has just the same love for us as he had for his first disciples. The bread and the wine, signs of his broken body and poured-out blood, remind us first and foremost of the extent of his love.

Picture the scene. Jesus begins to wash the feet of his disciples, and everyone watches with a hushed and shocked fascination. Before long, Jesus arrives at where Peter is sitting. Peter's reaction is to be embarrassed by his Master's display of love in this way, so much so that he draws back. As he says in verse 8: 'No, you shall never wash my feet', only to hear Jesus say, 'Unless I wash you, you have no part with me.' People find it intensely embarrassing to face up to their own needs. We would so like the boot to be on the other foot, so to speak – for *us* to be able to do something for *him*. But that comes later. We need always to begin with what *he* does for *us*. This is the second point about Holy Communion that this incident brings out. It shows us ourselves – and in a rather dim light. As we saw earlier, this meal illustrates both our need of forgiveness and the fact that such forgiveness is possible. To receive the bread and the wine is to accept what Jesus says and to admit that he is right: 'My body – broken for *you*. My blood – poured out for *your* forgiveness.' The vital importance of receiving as well as giving is even shown by Jesus himself. In the previous chapter, John records an event in which '. . . Mary took about a pint of pure nard, an expensive perfume; she poured it on Jesus' feet and wiped his feet with her hair. And the house was filled with the fragrance of the perfume' (John 12:3). The implication is clear: those who would love others must also allow themselves to be loved.

And so, thirdly, this story brings out the example of Jesus' love. In this simple action of washing the disciples' feet, Jesus shows not only how much he loves them, but also how much he wants them to love one another. 'I have set you an example that you should do as I have done for you', he tells them in John 13:15. This too has its counterpart in the meal of Holy Communion. For as Christians remember Jesus saying 'My life, given for you', so they're invited to respond as an act of worship, 'My life, Lord, given for you. My life at your disposal. My life available for you to live through.' Holy Communion is not only an act of remembering. It's also an act of worship, a communion between Jesus and his people, as they offer themselves afresh to the Lord who loves them and invites their love in response:

*   *   *

Take my life and let it be
all you purpose, Lord, for me;
consecrate my passing days,
let them flow in ceaseless praise.

*Take my hands, and let them move
at the impulse of your love;
take my feet, and let them run
with the news of victory won.*

*Take my voice, and let me sing
always, only, for my King;
take my lips, let them proclaim
all the beauty of your name.*

*Take my wealth, all I possess,
make me rich in faithfulness;
take my mind that I may use
every power as you shall choose.*

*Take my motives and my will,
all your purpose to fulfil;
take my heart — it is your own,
it shall be your royal throne.*

*Take my love — my Lord, I pour
at your feet its treasure-store;
take myself, and I will be
yours for all eternity.*

(Frances Ridley Havergal, 1836–79)[4]

*   *   *

Recognising Jesus

The idea that this meal together provides a special focus for such communion between us and Jesus also comes across in another incident, one of the most poignant and beautiful stories in the Gospels. The action takes place on the same day that the tomb of Jesus has been found to be empty, on the third day after his crucifixion and burial:

13Now that same day two of them were going to a village called Emmaus, about seven miles from Jerusalem. 14They were talking with each other about everything that had happened. 15As they talked and discussed these things with each other, Jesus himself came up and walked along with them; 16but they were kept from recognising him. 17He asked them, 'What are you discussing together as you walk along?' They stood still, their faces downcast. 18One of them, named Cleopas, asked him, 'Are you only a visitor to Jerusalem and do not know the things that have happened there in these days?' 19'What things?' he asked. 'About Jesus of Nazareth,' they replied. 'He was a prophet, powerful in word and deed before God and all the people. 20The chief priests and our rulers handed him over to be sentenced to death, and they crucified him; 21but we had hoped that he was the one who was going to redeem Israel. And what is more, it is the third day since all this took place. 22In addition, some of our women amazed us. They went to the tomb early this morning 23but didn't find his body. They came and told us that they had seen a vision of angels, who said he was alive. 24Then some of our companions went to the tomb and found it just as the women had said, but him they did not see.' 25He said to them, 'How foolish you are, and how slow of heart to believe all that the prophets have spoken! 26Did not the Christ have to suffer these things and then enter his glory?' 27And beginning with Moses and all the Prophets, he explained to them what was said in all the Scriptures concerning himself. 28As they approached the village to which they were going, Jesus acted as if he were going further. 29But they urged him strongly, 'Stay with us, for it is nearly evening; the day is almost over.' So he went in to stay with them. 30When he was at the table with them, he took bread, gave thanks, broke it and began to give it to them. 31Then their eyes were opened and they recognised him, and he disappeared from their sight. 32They asked each other, 'Were not our hearts burning within us while he talked with us on the road and opened the Scriptures to us?' 33They got up and returned at once to Jerusalem. There they found the Eleven and those with them, assembled together 34and saying, 'It is true! The Lord has risen and has appeared to Simon.' 35Then the two told what had happened on the way, and how Jesus was recognised by them when he broke the bread.

(Luke 24:13–35)

Notice what the risen Jesus chooses to do here. His main priority is to encourage the two disciples to focus on the fact that what has happened to him has all been foretold in the Scriptures. How much confusion and heartache they could have saved themselves! This is true for today's worshippers as well – reading, hearing and seeking to understand the Bible is a vital part of worship, not least when they gather to celebrate Holy Communion. There should be the expectation that, like the two disciples returning to Emmaus, hearts will be set on fire as Jesus unfolds the truths of his words through the power of his living Holy Spirit working both in those who speak and those who hear. As a preacher myself, nothing is more encouraging than to know that members of the congregation are praying that this will indeed happen as we gather together. One thing that will help here is if, instead of coming to the day's Bible readings 'cold', as it were, those attending a service have looked through them before coming to church and already begun to think about them and chew over what they mean.

Despite being tired after their journey and the trauma of the previous few days, Cleopas and his companion make a priority of offering hospitality to the stranger who has been walking with them. During the meal they suddenly realise who he is. As they tell the astonished disciples when they rush back into Jerusalem, the point at which they recognised Jesus was when he broke the bread. Christians down the years have expressed similar sentiments with the sense that Jesus is specially present when his death is being remembered in the way he prescribed.

Of course, Jesus promised his disciples, '. . . surely I am

with you always, to the very end of the age' (Matthew 28:20), and there's an important sense in which, through his Holy Spirit, Jesus is never absent from his followers. Nevertheless, there are circumstances in which people are perhaps more conscious of his presence than at other times. As we noted above, Jesus told his followers on another occasion: 'For where two or three come together in my name, there am I with them' (Matthew 18:20).

* * *

Come, risen Lord, and deign to be our guest;
nay, let us be thy guests; the feast is thine;
thyself at thine own board make manifest,
in thine own sacrament of bread and wine.

We meet, as in that upper room they met;
thou at the table, blessing, yet dost stand;
'This is my body': so thou givest yet;
faith still receives the cup as from thy hand.

One body we, one body who partake,
one church united in communion blest;
one name we bear, one bread of life we break,
with all thy saints on earth and saints at rest.

One with each other, Lord, for one in thee,
who art one Saviour and one living Head;
then open thou our eyes, that we may see;
be known to us in breaking of the bread.

(G. W. Briggs, 1875–1959)[5]

* * *

Present – and correct?

Exactly *how* Jesus is present at Holy Communion is a question that has divided Christians for centuries. The main lines of thought are as follows.

Historically, the Roman Catholic Church has held to the doctrine called *transubstantiation*, first proposed by Paschasius Radbertus in the ninth century. This was set out formally in 1215 at the Fourth Lateran Council and reaffirmed during the Council of Trent in the sixteenth century. Transubstantiation is the belief that as the priest repeats the words of Jesus, 'This is my body' and 'This is my blood', a miracle occurs in which the elements, though still *appearing* to be bread and wine, actually *become* the body and blood of Christ. As such, they are adored by the congregation and offered to God in the sacrifice of the Mass (the term Roman Catholics use for Holy Communion).

Of course, this doctrine didn't suddenly appear out of the blue. Its roots can be traced right back to the teachings of those men we call the 'Church Fathers' in the first few centuries after the New Testament era.[6] Whether or not such writers meant their readers to understand what was later formulated as the doctrine of transubstantiation is a matter for debate. And even if they did, this doesn't necessarily settle the question. Many of the disputes between Christians today stem from opposing views about the authority of these early writers. Those at the Catholic end of the spectrum tend to view these early writers' teaching as an extension of the Bible, and thus binding on succeeding generations. Those at the Protestant end of the spectrum regard what these writers say rather more loosely, and view the Bible alone as authoritative. This means that these early writers need not be right – indeed, if what they say contradicts the Bible, they *cannot* be right!

Transubstantiation was one of the doctrines rejected by most of the leaders of the Protestant Reformation in the sixteenth century. They saw it as something that goes against the clear teaching of Scripture and so must be abandoned. A number of alternatives were put forward to replace it. The German Reformer Martin Luther (1483–1546) held a view (sometimes referred to as *consubstantiation*) in which the bread and wine do not change, but the real presence of Jesus comes alongside them so that the consecrated elements are both bread and wine *and* the body and blood of Christ. This was too much for Swiss Reformer Huldreich Zwingli

(1484–1531), who considered that Luther was mistaken. How could Christ be divided – present both in the glory of heaven and in earthly bread and wine? He believed that when Jesus said, 'This is my body . . .', he meant, 'This *represents* my body . . .', and so Zwingli held that the bread and wine are simply symbols to help believers remember the significance of Jesus' death. In this view, known as *receptionism*, the presence of Christ is not to be located in the elements of bread and wine, but in the hearts of those who receive them in faith. In other words, just eating the bread and drinking the wine do not necessarily mean that someone has truly received the body and blood of Christ. In an attempt to mediate between Lutheran and Zwinglian views, the solution of John Calvin (1509–64) was to affirm that Jesus really is received when the bread and the wine are consumed, but that his presence is mediated by the Holy Spirit. For Calvin, the presence of Christ does not need to be localised to the bread and the wine. What happens when believers eat the bread and drink the wine is that the power of the Spirit unites them, body and soul, with the living Christ in heaven.

In churches today, each of the above views has its supporters, together with a wide range of subtle variations. It may come as some consolation to know that even the bishops of the Anglican Communion, meeting at the Lambeth Conference in 1988, concluded that the question of the presence of Christ in Holy Communion was one of a number of 'areas of "mystery" which ultimately defy definition'. However, that's not to say we should not try. In seeking to express truths about God, Christian theology is bound to find that its way of putting things is inadequate. But it's also important to note that, as today's Christians re-evaluate the context in which these debates have taken place in the past, there is scope for past divisions to be healed. In particular, much useful discussion has taken place in the context of ecumenical bodies (bodies that represent the *whole* Christian Church) like the Anglican–Roman Catholic International Commission (ARCIC), whose *Agreed Statement on Eucharistic Doctrine* was published in 1971. In recent years, some Roman Catholic theologians have drawn back from affirming the *physical* change in the bread and the wine implied by the word 'transubstantiation', and have spoken instead of 'transignification', whereby the bread and the wine receive a new purpose or significance – that of mediating the reality of the body and blood of Christ to those who receive them in faith.

*   *   *

Lord Jesus Christ,
we humbly thank you that you chose bread and wine
to be the emblems of your body and blood,
given on the cross for our sins,
and that you commanded us to remember you in this way.
Deepen our repentance,
strengthen our faith
and increase our love for one another, so that,
eating and drinking this sacrament of our redemption,
we may truly feed on you in our hearts by faith
with thanksgiving,
for the sake of your great and worthy name. Amen.[7]

*   *   *

Giving thanks

In all Christian worship, and perhaps especially in the service of Holy Communion, Christians commune with a living Lord, one whom they can thank personally, one-to-one, for the immense love that the bread and the wine signify. This is what lies behind the use of the noun 'Eucharist' (from the Greek for 'thanksgiving') to describe Holy Communion. Although the noun 'Eucharist' is not actually used in the New Testament, the corresponding verb 'to give thanks' certainly is, often in association with the action of breaking bread (e.g., Matthew 26:26–7; Luke 24:30; Acts 27:35; 1 Corinthians 11:24). The same term is used widely in the literature of the early Church and also by many Christians today.

True worship: God reveals

The best way to thank God is by responding in whole-hearted worship. It's worth thinking a little about what this means. First, true worship is always triggered by God himself. It isn't a feeling that people have to try and work up, but a response to what God reveals about himself. The job of the worshippers is simply to place themselves in the firing line of what God has to say. A good example of this comes in Paul's letter to the Romans: 'Therefore, I urge you, brothers, in view of God's mercy, to offer your bodies as living sacrifices, holy and pleasing to God – this is your spiritual act of worship' (Romans 12:1). This appeal to worship doesn't come out of the blue. It begins with, 'Therefore . . . in view of God's mercy'. Paul seeks to stimulate his readers to worship on the basis of what he has been telling them about God's mercy in the first eleven chapters of this letter. Worship, he tells his readers, is to be built on the foundation of what a merciful and gracious God has said and done. This is exactly what happens in Holy Communion as those taking part reflect, first on the word of God in the Bible and then on the work of Christ on the cross, graphically portrayed in the breaking of bread and pouring out of wine.

For it is only as God reveals himself that a response is possible. Like mirrors, worshippers can only reflect back to God the light of his truth that they have received. As the Bible itself reminds us, 'We love because he first loved us' (1 John 4:19). One of the fundamental truths about God is that he who would otherwise be quite beyond our reach chooses to make himself known. The first half of Psalm 19 illustrates how God does this through creation:

1The heavens declare the glory of God;
   the skies proclaim the work of his hands.
2Day after day they pour forth speech;
   night after night they display knowledge.
3There is no speech or language where their voice is not
   heard.
4Their voice goes out into all the earth,
   their words to the ends of the world.

In the heavens he has pitched a tent for the sun,
5which is like a bridegroom coming forth from his pavilion,
    like a champion rejoicing to run his course.
6It rises at one end of the heavens
    and makes its circuit to the other;
    nothing is hidden from its heat.

(Psalm 19:1–6)

In the second half of the Psalm, the focus shifts from the work of
God in creation to the word of God expressed in his laws:

7The law of the LORD is perfect,
    reviving the soul.
The statutes of the LORD are trustworthy,
    making wise the simple.
8The precepts of the LORD are right,
    giving joy to the heart.
The commands of the LORD are radiant,
    giving light to the eyes.
9The fear of the LORD is pure,
    enduring for ever.
The ordinances of the LORD are sure
    and altogether righteous.
10They are more precious than gold,
    than much pure gold;
    they are sweeter than honey,
    than honey from the comb.
11By them is your servant warned;
    in keeping them there is great reward.

12Who can discern his errors?
    Forgive my hidden faults.
13Keep your servant also from wilful sins;
    may they not rule over me.
Then will I be blameless,
    innocent of great transgression.

14May the words of my mouth and the meditation of my
  heart
  be pleasing in your sight,
  O LORD , my Rock and my Redeemer.

(Psalm 19:7–14)

In the New Testament, the writer to the Hebrews takes up
this theme of how God makes himself known at the beginning of
his epistle:

1In the past God spoke to our forefathers through the
prophets at many times and in various ways, 2but in these
last days he has spoken to us by his Son, whom he appoint-
ed heir of all things, and through whom he made the uni-
verse. 3The Son is the radiance of God's glory and the exact
representation of his being, sustaining all things by his powerful word. After he had provided purification for sins, he
sat down at the right hand of the Majesty in heaven.

(Hebrews 1:1–3)

God reveals himself through what he has made and by
speaking through his servants in the writings preserved for us in
the Bible. But his supreme act of self-disclosure was in the person of his Son, Jesus. Creation gives us important clues about
God's nature, and the Bible is his marvellous gift to us so that we
may discover in more depth what he is like. And this not least
because, as God's written word, it tells us so much about our Lord
and Saviour Jesus Christ, God's 'Word' born into the world as a
human being.

The beginning of John's Gospel makes the astonishing
claim that 'The Word became flesh and made his dwelling among
us. We have seen his glory, the glory of the One and Only, who
came from the Father, full of grace and truth' (John 1:14). Jesus
is the *Word* of God to show us what he is like and also, as John
mentions later in the same chapter, the *Lamb* of God to die for our
sins on the cross. These are the two dimensions on which Chris-

tians focus in Holy Communion: Jesus the Word of God revealed
in the Bible, and Jesus the Lamb of God revealed in the broken
bread and the poured-out wine. Word and sacrament together
bring us face to face with the God of grace and mercy who is worthy of all the worship and honour we can give.

*   *   *

Thank you for the cross,
the price you paid for us;
how you gave yourself so completely.
Precious Lord,
now our sins are gone, all forgiven,
covered by your blood; all forgotten –
thank you Lord.

Oh I love you, Lord, really love you, Lord.
I will never understand why you love me.
You're my deepest joy,
you're my heart's delight,
and the greatest thing of all, O Lord, I see –
you delight in me!

For our healing there,
Lord, you suffered;
and to take our fear you poured out your love.
Precious Lord,
Calvary's work is done, you have conquered;
able now to save so completely –
thank you Lord.

(Graham Kendrick)[8]

*   *   *

True worship: we respond

But what sort of response is God looking for? Look again at
Romans 12:1. To express what Paul means, he uses the picture of
sacrifice. When we use the word 'sacrifice' in general conversation,

we often talk about 'making a great sacrifice' to go and do the shopping or clean up the mess on the kitchen floor. In other words, a sacrifice *costs* us something. The idea of cost is certainly present in the biblical concept of sacrifice, as when King David refuses to 'sacrifice a burnt offering that costs me nothing' (1 Chronicles 21:24). Yet in the Bible, sacrifices are not made by people to one another, but specifically to God in order to please him.

In the Old Testament, there are basically two types of sacrifice, one negative and one positive. On the negative side, where people displeased God through their unbelief and disobedience, sacrifices were offered to appease his anger. God and his people, separated by sin, would be brought together again by the transfer of guilt to the sacrificial victim. Atonement (i.e., at-one-ment) would be made. On the positive side, sacrifices would be offered in joyful thanksgiving for God's goodness, especially at harvest times.

But it's different for Christians today who live in the period of history after the ministry of Jesus on earth. Because of his death, the first sort of sacrifice is unnecessary; the time for having to offer animal sacrifices for sin is now over. Jesus, by his death, has made that sacrifice once and for all. This is a major theme of the New Testament letter to the Hebrews, which contrasts the completed perfection of what Jesus achieved on the cross with the temporary effect of the sacrifices offered under the Old Testament system.

In the history of Christian worship, those towards the Catholic end of the spectrum have sought to associate Christ's offering of himself on the cross with the church's offering of the bread and the wine in Holy Communion. This has sometimes led to the idea that Christ is repeatedly sacrificed in order to appease God's anger, a statement that directly contradicts the teaching of the New Testament (e.g. Hebrews 7:27; 9:25–8; 10:10–18) and was specifically denied by the Anglican–Roman Catholic International Commission in the *Agreed Statement on Eucharistic Doctrine* of 1971: 'Christ's death on the cross, the culmination of his whole life of obedience, was the one, perfect and sufficient sacrifice for the sins of the world. There can be no repetition of or addition to what was accomplished once for all by Christ'.[9]

But some still want to speak of Christ's sacrifice being, if not repeated, then *perpetuated* or *represented* in Holy Communion as a reflection of the fact that Jesus is said to be continuously offering himself to the Father. The difficulty is that this represents a diversion from the clear teaching of the New Testament. Christ's offering of himself was a once-for-all event rather than a continuous process. Heaven contains his throne, but not his altar. He is certainly an eternal priest (see, for example, Hebrews 7:24–8) who intercedes for us at God's right hand, but he is not an eternal victim.

Another suggestion has been that Holy Communion is a means whereby Christians, as members of Christ's body, share in the offering of Christ of himself as our head. But again, the danger is that this compromises the uniqueness of Christ's offering of himself on the cross. As we shall see, it *is* appropriate to speak of our offering sacrifices in our worship, but such sacrifices are made 'through' Christ (e.g. 1 Peter 2:5), not 'with' him. He is the *object* of our worship, not one who worships *with* us.

But even if we need to be cautious about suggestions that we share in Christ's offering of himself, there is still plenty of scope for offering sacrifices of thanks and praise. Just what does this mean, though? Given that teaching the skill of butcher is no longer on the syllabus of our theological colleges and that today's ministers are not expected to slaughter large quantities of livestock, what sort of sacrifices *do* Christian worshippers offer? The answer is that they offer what the Bible calls *spiritual* sacrifices. Let's look at some of the things that the Bible teaches about this.

Spiritual sacrifices

To begin with, we go back to Romans 12:1 once again: 'Therefore, I urge you, brothers, in view of God's mercy, to offer your bodies as living sacrifices, holy and pleasing to God – this is your spiritual act of worship.' A 'living sacrifice' sounds like a contradiction in terms, but what Paul has in mind is that the way Christians live their lives – what they do with their own bodies rather than the bodies of sacrificial animals – is to be their act of worship. This underlines once again that worship is not just something that takes place during services in church on Sundays. It also emphasises that worship is much more than simply experiencing warm feelings about God. To *feel* good is fine – but not if it distracts us from the need to *be* good as well! Worship is about the whole of life.

As an example of this, here's how Paul commends some of the churches he had been in touch with. They had been enthusiastic to give financial support to their fellow believers who were known to be in need, and so he writes this about them: 'Entirely on their own, they urgently pleaded with us for the privilege of sharing in this service to the saints. And they did not do as we expected, but *they gave themselves first to the Lord* and then to us in keeping with God's will' (2 Corinthians 8:4–5, my italics). This is the key to true worship: the giving of ourselves, lock, stock and barrel, to God. At certain points in history and in certain parts of the world even today, such giving extends to Christians literally laying down their lives because of their loyalty to their Lord. This is something all Christian worshippers need to bear in mind as a possibility – however unlikely a prospect it may seem to be at the moment.

What is usually called 'worship', the outward vocal expression of love for God, is important, but is simply the icing on the cake. True worship has cake as well. True worshippers know that icing brings out the flavour of the cake but that icing with no cake to support it is liable to give God indigestion!

God invites those who come to him in worship to offer themselves, all that they are. And Holy Communion is an especially appropriate time during which to renew such an offering.

*   *   *

Our Father, who art in heaven,
hallowed be thy name;
thy kingdom come;
thy will be done;
on earth as it is in heaven.
Give us this day our daily bread.
And forgive us our trespasses,
as we forgive those who trespass against us.
And lead us not into temptation;
but deliver us from evil.
For thine is the kingdom, the power, and the glory,
for ever and ever.
Amen.
(The traditional form of the Lord's Prayer)

Our Father in heaven,
hallowed be your name,
your kingdom come,
your will be done,
on earth as in heaven.
Give us today our daily bread.
Forgive us our sins
as we forgive those who sin against us.
Lead us not into temptation
but deliver us from evil.
For the kingdom, the power, and the glory are yours
now and for ever. Amen.
(The version of the Lord's Prayer used in the Church of
England's *Alternative Service Book 1980*)

*   *   *

Praise and prayer

Here are some quotations from the Bible that highlight
some of the outward expressions of worship:

I will praise God's name in song and glorify him with thanksgiving. This will please the LORD more than an ox, more than a bull with its horns and hoofs.

(Psalm 69:30–1)

May my prayer be set before you like incense; may the lifting up of my hands be like the evening sacrifice.

(Psalm 141:2)

. . . golden bowls full of incense, which are the prayers of the saints.

(Revelation 5:8)

Through Jesus, therefore, let us continually offer to God a sacrifice of praise – the fruit of lips that confess his name.

(Hebrews 13:15)

Throughout history, music has had an important part to play in worship as God's people express their praises and offer their prayers. This is no accident. To *say* something to God is one thing, but to *sing* it adds a totally new dimension. Music enables us to express much more fully the depth and variety of what we feel. Jesus indicated that the 'first and greatest commandment' is to 'love the Lord your God with all your heart and with all your soul and with all your mind' (Matthew 22:37), something that music is intended to help us to do more fully, whether through singing or playing a musical instrument, whether on our own or with others:

1Praise the LORD.
  Praise God in his sanctuary;
  praise him in his mighty heavens.
2Praise him for his acts of power;
  praise him for his surpassing greatness.
3Praise him with the sounding of the trumpet,
  praise him with the harp and lyre,

4praise him with tambourine and dancing,
    praise him with the strings and flute,
5praise him with the clash of cymbals,
    praise him with resounding cymbals.
6Let everything that has breath praise the LORD.
    Praise the LORD.

                                    (Psalm 150)

Music is a powerful way of binding a group of people together in worship as their diverse contributions are united in a (hopefully!) harmonious whole. Of course, there are dangers: music can all too easily become an end in itself, and so become a tyrannical distraction to true worship rather than its servant. That which is intended to unite Christians in worship can easily become a cause of division between those whose musical tastes and levels of skill differ. This is one of the reasons why great care needs to be taken when a service of worship is being planned. Even if not everything is to everyone's taste, no one should feel completely excluded and so unable to participate.

             *   *   *

Glory be to God on high,
and in earth, peace, good will towards men.
We praise thee, we bless thee,
we worship thee, we glorify thee,
we give thanks to thee for thy great glory,
O Lord God, heavenly King, God the Father Almighty.

O Lord, the only-begotten Son Jesu Christ;
O Lord God, Lamb of God, Son of the Father,
that takest away the sins of the world,
have mercy upon us.
Thou that takest away the sins of the world,
have mercy upon us.

Thou that takest away the sins of the world,
receive our prayer.
Thou that sittest at the right hand of God the Father,
have mercy upon us.

For thou only art holy; thou only art the Lord;
thou only, O Christ, with the Holy Spirit,
art most high in the glory of God the Father.
*Amen.*10

*   *   *

When things are tough

Sometimes, these external expressions of worship come easily, but not always. On occasions, worship can feel like a real sacrifice and be a really costly undertaking. It sometimes takes an effort to rise above depressing circumstances and worship God for who he is in spite of them. However, this should not come as any great surprise. Indeed, the more difficult worship seems to be and the more it seems to cost, then perhaps the more precious it is to God. The wonderful example of the Old Testament prophet Habakkuk is a great one to learn from. He lets his imagination run riot as he thinks up a whole range of disasters that might happen to him. Or perhaps they already have! He then affirms, though, that he has no intention of letting these disasters deflect him from worshipping God: 'Though the fig-tree does not bud and there are no grapes on the vines, though the olive crop fails and the fields produce no food, though there are no sheep in the pen and no cattle in the stalls, yet will I rejoice in the LORD, I will be joyful in God my Saviour. The Sovereign LORD is my strength; he makes my feet like the feet of a deer, he enables me to go on the heights' (Habakkuk 3:17–19).

Or take the example of Job, another character in the Old Testament. One day, a messenger comes to tell him that raiders have carried off all his oxen and donkeys and killed the servants looking after them. Only this particular messenger has been able to escape to tell Job the news. While he is still speaking, another messenger comes to report the loss of all Job's sheep. Then another comes to tell him that all his camels have been taken from him. Finally, another brings news that even his sons and daughters have perished. Apart from the four messengers who bring the terrible news, Job has only his wife left – and, as the Bible shows, it has to be admitted that his wife proves to be something of a mixed blessing! So how does Job respond to all this? 'At this, Job got up and tore his robe and shaved his head [a mark of mourning]. Then he fell to the ground in worship and said "Naked I came from my mother's womb, and naked I shall depart. The LORD gave and the LORD has taken away; may the name of the LORD be praised"' (Job 1:20–1). Even while facing such a sequence of disasters, Job remains firm in his commitment to worship God.

The same attitude is found in the New Testament too. Given the circumstances under which it was written, we might expect that Paul's letter to the Philippians would be one of the most depressing in the New Testament. Locked up in prison and facing the prospect of imminent execution, Paul could perhaps have been excused if he didn't really feel like expressing his desire to worship. But no, the book of Philippians overflows with Paul's enthusiasm for his Lord, and the repeated encouragement to rise above even the most dire circumstances and to praise God – not necessarily *for* these circumstances, but certainly *in* them: 'Rejoice in the Lord always. I will say it again: Rejoice! Let your gentleness be evident to all. The Lord is near. Do not be anxious about anything, but in everything, by prayer and petition, with thanksgiving, present your requests to God. And the peace of God, which transcends all understanding, will guard your hearts and your minds in Christ Jesus' (Philippians 4:4–7).

Confessing sin

I used to think that the Confession (said by the congregation) and Absolution (said by the minister) were rather odd things to have in the *middle* of a service of worship. Surely they need to be got out of the way before things get going! In one sense, that's true, and many services do have a section devoted to penitence near the beginning of the service. But how about this verse from one of the Psalms? 'You do not delight in sacrifice, or I would bring it; you do not take pleasure in burnt offerings. The sacrifices of God are a broken spirit; a broken and contrite heart, O God, you will not despise' (Psalm 51:16–17).

This is God's glorious encouragement for worshippers to be themselves in worship, to come to him as they are, in all their weakness and failure. As someone once put it, 'A Christian is not one who never sins, but one who when he sins does not lose his confidence in God but repents and continues the fight.' The constant ploy of the devil is to drive people away from fellowship with God by persuading them that, because they are unworthy, they don't belong. The truth is that, yes, we are unworthy, but, as Holy Communion proclaims loud and clear, we *can* belong because of the worth of another: our Saviour, Jesus Christ. Therefore repentance is an important ingredient in worship.

Helping others
We saw earlier how worship involves the whole of life. Here's this idea fleshed out in another direction: 'And do not forget to do good and to share with others, for with such sacrifices God is pleased' (Hebrews 13:16). This is a point that comes over in Paul's letters too: '. . . I have received from Epaphroditus the gifts you sent. They are a fragrant offering, an acceptable sacrifice, pleasing to God' (Philippians 4:18). In other words, showing practical love for other people is seen as one of the ways we can express our love for God. John goes even further in his first letter by saying that it's only as they truly love *one another* that Christians can justify the claim that they love *God*:

7Dear friends, let us love one another, for love comes from God. Everyone who loves has been born of God and knows God. 8Whoever does not love does not know God, because God is love. 9This is how God showed his love among us: He sent his one and only Son into the world that we might live through him. 10This is love: not that we loved God, but that he loved us and sent his Son as an atoning sacrifice for our sins. [11]Dear friends, since God so loved us, we also ought to love one another. [12]No-one has ever seen God; but if we love one another, God lives in us and his love is made complete in us . . .

[19]We love because he first loved us. [20]If anyone says, 'I love God,' yet hates his brother, he is a liar. For anyone who does not love his brother, whom he has seen, cannot love God, whom he has not seen. [21]And he has given us this command: Whoever loves God must also love his brother.
(1 John 4:7–12, 19–21)

Such love is reflected in services of Holy Communion in a number of different ways. For one thing, there is the offertory or collection, during which gifts of money are received from the congregation to be used both for the maintenance of the church's ministry and also to help those who are in need. As we saw earlier from the details of second-century services set out by Justin Martyr, this receiving of people's gifts in the context of Holy Communion has an ancient precedent. But it goes back even further than that. Here's what Paul has to say, this time to the Corinthians: 'On the first day of every week, each one of you should set aside a sum of money in keeping with his income, saving it up . . .' (1 Corinthians 16:2). The point is that the giving of money, far from being an intrusion into our worship, is a vital part of it. Christians need to be prepared and ready to offer their purses and wallets to God as much as anything else. Unlike the highwaymen who plagued travellers in the past, God invites us to hand over our money *and* our life! Exactly how much people give is up to them, of course, though notice that Paul specifies a weekly amount in proportion to our income. Many Christians use the Old Testament guideline of giving back to God a minimum ten per cent of what they receive, often known as a *tithe*. A tithe traditionally meant a tenth of something.

Paul returns to the theme in his second letter to the

Corinthians (chapter 9): 'Each man should give what he has decided in his heart to give, not reluctantly or under compulsion, for God loves a cheerful giver [verse 7]. And God is able to make all grace abound to you, so that in all things at all times, having all that you need, you will abound in every good work [verse 8]'. This emphasises the way in which worship, in this as in any other area, is not simply about our actions but about our underlying attitudes. Money can be sharply devalued by being given grudgingly. On the other hand, verse 8 comes as a wonderful promise for those who take the risk of putting verse 7 into practice. Try it and see!

Mission and evangelism

There's one final area of worship that we need to look at before moving on. One of the most surprising references to sacrifice comes towards the end of Paul's letter to the Romans. Paul is writing about his ministry of taking the good news to the Gentile population. God gave him grace, he wrote, 'to be a minister of Christ Jesus to the Gentiles with the priestly duty of proclaiming the gospel of God, so that the Gentiles might become an offering acceptable to God, sanctified by the Holy Spirit' (Romans 15:16–17). Paul considers his Christian witness to others in terms of offering a sacrifice. He sees his work of bringing the gospel to the Gentiles as an act of worship, and views those whom he has been able to bring to faith in Christ as part of what he offers to God. They too are part of his worship, and they can be part of ours as well.

* * *

> Deck yourself, my soul, with gladness;
> leave the gloomy haunts of sadness.
> Come into the daylight's splendour,
> there with joy your praises render
> to the Lord whose grace unbounded
> has this royal banquet founded:
> though all other powers excelling,
> with my soul he makes his dwelling.

Lord, I bow before you lowly,
filled with joy most deep and holy,
as with trembling awe and wonder
all your mighty works I ponder
how, by mystery surrounded,
depth no man has ever sounded,
none may dare to pierce unbidden
secrets that in you are hidden.

Shining sun, my life you brighten,
radiance, you my soul enlighten;
joy, the best of all man's knowing,
fountain, swiftly in me flowing:
at your feet I kneel, my Maker –
let me be a fit partaker
of this sacred food from heaven,
for our good, your glory, given.

Jesus, Bread of life, I pray you,
let me gladly here obey you;
never to my hurt invited,
always by your love delighted:
from this banquet let me measure,
Lord, how vast and deep its treasure;
through the gifts your hands have given
let me be your guest in heaven.

(After J. Franck, 1618–77)[11]

CHAPTER 6

🌿 Looking around
Fellowship and Holy Communion

IN THIS CHAPTER we shall focus on the fact that Holy Communion is a meal that Christians share *together*. This is one of the significant things about its roots in the Jewish Passover meal, which was essentially a family festival. Holy Communion isn't simply a solitary encounter with the Lord, although as we saw in the last chapter, it *is* an opportunity for Christians to renew their personal relationship with the Lord. Indeed, one of the most beautiful and evocative pictures of the relationship between Jesus and his individual followers comes in the book of Revelation: 'Here I am! I stand at the door and knock. If anyone hears my voice and opens the door, I will come in and eat with him, and he with me' (Revelation 3:20).

But Holy Communion is not *only* this. After all, people don't have such services on their own: Christians participate together in this meal. For example, the Church of England's *Book of Common Prayer* specifies that '. . . there shall be no Communion, except four (or three at the least) communicate with the Priest'.

True fellowship
To help us to understand this aspect, we'll have another look at what the apostle Paul has to say in his first letter to the church at Corinth. He is less than complimentary about what he sees as their abuse of Holy Communion:

[17]In the following directives I have no praise for you, for your meetings do more harm than good. [18]In the first place,

I hear that when you come together as a church, there are divisions among you, and to some extent I believe it. 19No doubt there have to be differences among you to show which of you have God's approval. 20When you come together, it is not the Lord's Supper you eat, 21for as you eat, each of you goes ahead without waiting for anybody else. One remains hungry, another gets drunk. 22Don't you have homes to eat and drink in? Or do you despise the church of God and humiliate those who have nothing? What shall I say to you? Shall I praise you for this? Certainly not! 23For I received from the Lord what I also passed on to you: The Lord Jesus, on the night he was betrayed, took bread, 24and when he had given thanks, he broke it and said, 'This is my body, which is for you; do this in remembrance of me.' 25In the same way, after supper he took the cup, saying, 'This cup is the new covenant in my blood; do this, whenever you drink it, in remembrance of me.' 26For whenever you eat this bread and drink this cup, you proclaim the Lord's death until he comes. 27Therefore, whoever eats the bread or drinks the cup of the Lord in an unworthy manner will be guilty of sinning against the body and blood of the Lord. 28A man ought to examine himself before he eats of the bread and drinks of the cup. 29For anyone who eats and drinks without recognising the body of the Lord eats and drinks judgment on himself. 30That is why many among you are weak and sick, and a number of you have fallen asleep. 31But if we judged ourselves, we would not come under judgment. 32When we are judged by the Lord, we are being disciplined so that we will not be condemned with the world. 33So then, my brothers, when you come together to eat, wait for each other. 34If anyone is hungry, he should eat at home, so that when you meet together it may not result in judgment. And when I come I will give further directions.

(1 Corinthians 11:17–34)

In Paul's mind, there is a close link between worthy participation in the bread and the wine on the one hand and the quality of relationships within the Christian community on the other. It's no good Christians trying simply to put right their 'vertical' relationship with God: their 'horizontal' relationships with one another are just as important. Jesus' advice about acceptable worship is relevant here: '. . . if you are offering your gift at the altar and there remember that your brother has something against you, leave your gift there in front of the altar. First go and be reconciled to your brother; then come and offer your gift' (Matthew 5:23–4).

Earlier in his first letter to the Corinthians, Paul includes this comment: 'Is not the cup of thanksgiving for which we give thanks a participation in the blood of Christ? And is not the bread that we break a participation in the body of Christ? Because there is one loaf, we, who are many, are one body, for we all partake of the one loaf' (1 Corinthians 10:16–17).

To partake together of one loaf and drink from the one cup is a very dramatic and striking way for Christians to express their unity with one another. Some forms of service express this verbally when the bread is broken by referring to what Paul says here: 'We break this bread to share in the body of Christ. Though we are many, we are one body, because we all share in one bread.' It's perhaps a pity that many churches, in seeking to make the administration of the bread and wine easier and more hygienic, undermine this powerful symbolism of unity, either by using individual wafers or individual communion cups. The following passage from a recent book illustrates the point that is being made:

. . . I come to the Eucharist, wondering what evidence of Jesus I will find. As I administer the bread, the first person at the communion rail is Amy, eighty years old. Next to her is three-year-old Carmen, waiting to receive a blessing. Her sticky fingers clutch a lollipop, while she swings on the rail. Brian, a thirty-year-old school teacher, is next to her. Then comes Harry. He can neither read nor write and lives in a squalid bedsitter. Debbie, a local journalist is next and then

William, the homeless alcoholic, followed by Susan, a single mum. Shoulder to shoulder with her is Paul an elec-
tronic engineer, followed by Ron, who has recently been
convicted of theft. Where Jesus is present and how he is
present in this Eucharist, is still a mystery to me. But, that
he is present is beyond doubt. Only Jesus of Nazareth could
gather together round one table such beautiful and diverse
people. The Lord is here and his presence is with us.[1]

'Bring and share'

From time to time, some churches today include a complete
meal with a celebration of Holy Communion, sometimes called an
agape meal (from one of the Greek words meaning 'love'). But it
seems that eating together was the rule rather than the exception
in New Testament times. Such gatherings would take place in the
homes of church members, for church buildings as we know them
today did not exist until the fourth century. In the Greek city of
Corinth, it's clear that (as we've already seen) Holy Communion
was being spoiled by divisions within the fellowship of believers.
In particular, people were being selfish and not thinking of others.
Instead of a 'bring and share' supper, some of them were indulging
in a purely 'bring' supper as they went ahead with their own meal
while others went hungry. Paul sees this as a travesty of what Holy
Communion is all about, for all come on the same level, as unde-
serving sinners, to the Lord's table. None is greater than the others. If we are Christians, then we are all brothers and sisters,
children of the same heavenly Father. There is no place for pride
and selfishness that looks down on others or ignores them.

Neither is there room for those whose relationships have
broken down for other reasons. A quotation from the 'small print'
(rubrics) of the Church of England's *Book of Common Prayer* spells
this out rather quaintly, but with impressive clarity:

. . . And if any of those be an open and notorious evil liver,
or have done any wrong to his neighbours by word or deed,
so that the Congregation be thereby offended; the Curate,

having knowledge thereof, shall call him and advertise him, that in any wise he presume not to come to the Lord's Table, until he have openly declared himself to have truly repented and amended his former naughty life, that the Congregation may thereby be satisfied, which before were offended; and that he have recompensed the parties, to whom he hath done wrong; or at least declare himself to be in full purpose so to do, as soon as he conveniently may. The same order shall the Curate use with those betwixt whom he perceiveth malice and hatred to reign; not suffering them to be partakers of the Lord's Table, until he know them to be reconciled . . .

Peace

Some orders of service include the formal recognition of this dimension of Holy Communion by including the 'Sharing of the Peace' with one another, a way of saying to one another, 'We all belong, we're among family.' Of course, it's no good just *saying* it – as was graphically highlighted by a report in *The Buffalo News*, an American newspaper, a few years ago: 'A handshake during a "greeting of peace" ceremony in a church service has resulted in a $100,000 lawsuit. Catherine Fritz, a real-estate broker, said the handshake of William Schleicher Jr. was not friendly. Her suit contends Mr Schleicher "did wilfully, wantonly, with malice, intent and with great force so grasp and seize" her right hand on March 22, 1977 . . .'

We need not just to *say* that we care, but to *show* it in practical ways as well – by positively helping one another, not merely avoiding doing one another harm when shaking hands! As we saw in the last chapter, this is an essential part of what worshipping God is all about. Luke brings this feature out in his description of the life of the early Church at the beginning of the Acts of the Apostles. It's likely that he is mentioning Holy Communion, using the term that some Christians still use today – 'the breaking of bread':

42They devoted themselves to the apostles' teaching and to the fellowship, to the breaking of bread and to prayer. 43Everyone was filled with awe, and many wonders and miraculous signs were done by the apostles. 44All the believers were together and had everything in common. 45Selling their possessions and goods, they gave to anyone as he had need. 46Every day they continued to meet together in the temple courts. They broke bread in their homes and ate together with glad and sincere hearts, 47praising God and enjoying the favour of all the people. And the Lord added to their number daily those who were being saved.

(Acts 2:42–7)

How much more vibrant the life of our churches would be if more of this were to be put into practice. Of course, it's true that there are important differences between life in the first century and life today, and it would be wrong to imitate slavishly what we read. But the principle of generosity that these verses describe is compelling and attractive. No wonder the Lord chose to add to their numbers!

*   *   *

Lord, make me an instrument of your peace.
Where there is hatred, let me bring love:
where there is injury, forgiveness:
where there is discord, unity:
where there is error, truth:
where there is doubt, faith:
where there is despair, hope:
where there is darkness, light:
where there is sadness, joy.
Divine Master,
help me not to seek so much
to be consoled, as to console:
to be understood, as to understand:
to be loved, as to love.

For it is in giving that we receive:
it is in forgiving that we are forgiven:
it is in dying that we are born again to eternal life.

(A prayer by St Francis of Assisi)

*   *   *

Intercession

Another way that Christians express their fellowship is in the act of praying together. Most services of Holy Communion include opportunities for intercession (praying for others), sometimes according to a set pattern, sometimes more informally and spontaneously. The cue for this comes from the apostle Paul: 'I urge, then, first of all, that requests, prayers, intercession and thanksgiving be made for everyone – for kings and all those in authority, that we may live peaceful and quiet lives in all godliness and holiness. This is good, and pleases God our Saviour, who wants all men to be saved and to come to a knowledge of the truth' (1 Timothy 2:1–4).

In other words, worshippers are not to pray simply for their own needs, or even just for the needs of fellow members of the congregation. These *are* prayed for, of course, but the perspective is much wider. Congregations also join in prayer for the world in general, especially for its leaders – just as Paul says here; and they join in praying for their brothers and sisters in the Church throughout the world, especially where they are known to be under particular pressure. Many churches have developed special links with those in other parts of the world and pray regularly for specific individuals, churches and mission agencies.

16I have not stopped giving thanks for you, remembering you in my prayers. 17I keep asking that the God of our Lord Jesus Christ, the glorious Father, may give you the Spirit of wisdom and revelation, so that you may know him better. 18I pray also that the eyes of your heart may be enlightened in order that you may know the hope to which he has called you, the riches of his glorious inheritance in the saints, [19]and his incomparably great power for us who believe . . .

(Ephesians 1:16–19)

[14]. . . I kneel before the Father, [15]from whom his whole family in heaven and on earth derives its name. [16]I pray that out of his glorious riches he may strengthen you with power through his Spirit in your inner being, [17]so that Christ may dwell in your hearts through faith. And I pray that you, being rooted and established in love, [18]may have power, together with all the saints, to grasp how wide and long and high and deep is the love of Christ, [19]and to know this love that surpasses knowledge – that you may be filled to the measure of all the fulness of God. [20]Now to him who is able to do immeasurably more than all we ask or imagine, according to his power that is at work within us, [21]to him be glory in the church and in Christ Jesus throughout all generations, for ever and ever! Amen.

(Ephesians 3:14–21)

Belief

A few years ago, I heard someone objecting to one of the changes that had been introduced into the modern Church of England prayer book. In the traditional much-loved *Book of Common Prayer*, the Creeds begin with a firm 'I believe . . .', but the new versions start with 'We believe . . .' instead. This particular individual was rather distressed at the change. 'How can I say "We believe",' he wanted to know, 'when I have no idea whether we all do or not?' My response was to suggest that the 'We' doesn't just mean the congregation gathered at that particular moment in that particular place. When we say 'We believe . . .' we are expressing the solidarity of faith that we share with our fellow Christians, not only all over the world but also throughout the last two thousand years.

*   *   *

We believe in one God,
the Father, the almighty,
maker of heaven and earth,
of all that is,
seen and unseen.

We believe in one Lord, Jesus Christ,
the only Son of God,
eternally begotten of the Father,
God from God, Light from Light,
true God from true God,
begotten, not made,
of one Being with the Father.
Through him all things were made.
For us men and for our salvation
he came down from heaven;
by the power of the Holy Spirit
he became incarnate of the Virgin Mary and was made man.
For our sake he was crucified under Pontius Pilate;
he suffered death and was buried.
On the third day he rose again
in accordance with the Scriptures;
he ascended into heaven
and is seated at the right hand of the Father.
He will come again in glory
to judge the living and the dead,
and his kingdom will have no end.

We believe in the Holy Spirit,
the Lord, the giver of life,
who proceeds from the Father and the Son.
With the Father and the Son he is worshipped and glorified.
He has spoken through the Prophets.
We believe in one holy catholic and apostolic Church.
We acknowledge one baptism for the forgiveness of sins.
We look for the resurrection of the dead,
and the life of the world to come. Amen.
(The Nicene Creed, from the *Alternative Service Book 1980*)

Many of the creeds recited regularly in churches today date right back to the early years of the Church, and very much reflect the style of the controversies of the time. If we were to write a creed for our own day (an interesting exercise, by the way – what do you think it would need to say?), it would probably be rather different, simply because the questions we face are different. For example, it would probably need to say something definitive about the authority of the Bible, a point that was taken for granted then, but is a rather more contentious issue now. But despite this, Christians still hold on to the statements of belief called the Apostles' Creed and the Nicene Creed. They give a sense of togetherness between an individual congregation and the rest of the Christian family throughout space and time.

* * *

I come with joy, a child of God,
forgiven, loved and free;
the life of Jesus to recall
in love laid down for me.

I come with Christians far and near
to find, as all are fed,
the new community of love
in Christ's communion bread.

As Christ breaks bread, and bids us share,
each proud division ends;
the love that made us, makes us one,
and strangers now are friends.

The Spirit of the risen Christ,
unseen, but ever near,
is in such friendship better known,
alive among us here.

Together met, together bound
by all that God has done,
we'll go with joy, to give the world
the love that makes us one.

(B. A. Wren, b. 1936)[2]

CHAPTER 7

🌹 Looking forward
The future in Holy Communion

He gave his life in selfless love,
for sinners once he came;
he had no stain of sin himself
but bore our guilt and shame:
he took the cup of pain and death,
his blood was freely shed;
we see his body on the cross,
we share the living bread.

He did not come to call the good
but sinners to repent;
it was the lame, the deaf, the blind
for whom his life was spent:
to heal the sick, to find the lost —
it was for such he came,
and round his table all may come
to praise his holy name.

They heard him call his Father's name —
then 'Finished!' was his cry;
like them we have forsaken him
and left him there to die:
the sins that crucified him then
are sins his blood has cured;
the love that bound him to a cross
our freedom has ensured.

His body broken once for us
is glorious now above;
the cup of blessing we receive,
a sharing of his love:
as in his presence we partake,
his dying we proclaim
until the hour of majesty
when Jesus comes again.

(C. Porteous, b. 1935)[1]

*   *   *

AS WE'VE SEEN, those celebrating the Jewish Passover festival in Jesus' day looked back to God's act of rescuing his people in the past. It was, above everything else, an act of remembrance, but it also came to have a future dimension. Under pressure from a variety of hostile forces – not least, in Jesus' day, the Roman Empire – God's people looked forward to what he would do to rescue them through the coming of the Messiah, a supernatural figure who would restore the fortunes of Israel.

Even after being with Jesus for three years, the disciples couldn't quite get this idea about restoring the fortunes of Israel out of their minds. At the beginning of the Acts of the Apostles, Luke records their question to Jesus shortly before he returned to heaven after his resurrection:

6. . . when they met together, they asked him, 'Lord, are you at this time going to restore the kingdom to Israel?' 7He said to them: 'It is not for you to know the times or dates the Father has set by his own authority. 8But you will receive power when the Holy Spirit comes on you; and you will be my witnesses in Jerusalem, and in all Judea and Samaria, and to the ends of the earth.' 9After he said this, he was taken up before their very eyes, and a cloud hid him from their sight. 10They were looking intently up into the sky as he was going, when suddenly two men dressed in

white stood beside them. [11]'Men of Galilee,' they said, 'why do you stand here looking into the sky? This same Jesus, who has been taken from you into heaven, will come back in the same way you have seen him go into heaven.'

(Acts 1:6–11)

The New Testament makes it very clear that the final abolition of all that runs counter to God's will is certainly on the divine agenda. But, as the above passage shows, God is interested in dealing properly with the problems that have beset the whole world throughout history, not just tinkering with those that faced the nation of Israel in the first century. One day, Jesus will return as Judge to put things right once and for all. Meanwhile, his followers are not to stand gawping at the clouds, but to get on with the job he has given them – the focus here being the particular task of telling people all over the world about him and the rescue plan he has brought into being.

As the years go by, this return of Christ to usher in the final rule of God can sometimes seem to be a rather forlorn hope. It's here that the perspective of another New Testament writer can help us:

[3]First of all, you must understand that in the last days scoffers will come, scoffing and following their own evil desires. [4]They will say, 'Where is this "coming" he promised? Ever since our fathers died, everything goes on as it has since the beginning of creation.' . . .

[8]But do not forget this one thing, dear friends: With the Lord a day is like a thousand years, and a thousand years are like a day. [9]The Lord is not slow in keeping his promise, as some understand slowness. He is patient with you, not wanting anyone to perish, but everyone to come to repentance. [10]But the day of the Lord will come like a thief. The heavens will disappear with a roar; the elements will be destroyed by fire, and the earth and everything in it will be

laid bare. [11]Since everything will be destroyed in this way, what kind of people ought you to be? You ought to live holy and godly lives [12]as you look forward to the day of God and speed its coming. That day will bring about the destruction of the heavens by fire, and the elements will melt in the heat. [13]But in keeping with his promise we are looking forward to a new heaven and a new earth, the home of righteousness. [14]So then, dear friends, since you are looking forward to this, make every effort to be found spotless, blameless and at peace with him.

(2 Peter 3:3–4, 8–14)

This dimension of future hope is also reflected in the Gospel accounts of the Last Supper, and so is an important part of what Christians celebrate when they join together in Holy Communion. Here's how Mark describes this aspect: 'Then he took the cup, gave thanks and offered it to them, and they all drank from it. "This is my blood of the covenant, which is poured out for many," he said to them. "I tell you the truth, I will not drink again of the fruit of the vine until that day when I drink it anew in the kingdom of God"' (Mark 14:23–5).

Luke records Jesus saying this: '"... I have eagerly desired to eat this Passover with you before I suffer. For I tell you, I will not eat it again until it finds fulfilment in the kingdom of God." After taking the cup, he gave thanks and said, "Take this and divide it among you. For I tell you I will not drink again of the fruit of the vine until the kingdom of God comes."' (Luke 22:15–18).

For Jesus, the Last Supper he had with his disciples looked forward to something else – the full and final arrival of the kingdom of God, when his rule will be established and evil will be permanently overcome. He told his followers to repeat what he did with the bread and the wine in anticipation that one day they would once again eat and drink with Jesus. Of course, there would be important differences. At the Last Supper, there were just a few of them in a room in Jerusalem. But with the coming of the kingdom of God, the feast will be in the glory of heaven with multitudes of believers from every age and every part of the world. Christians affirm their share in this hope as they continue to celebrate Holy Communion.

The circumstances in which Christians eat the bread and drink the wine are sometimes tough and hard to bear. Day by day we face the struggle against sin, both in our own lives and in the world around us. We are under constant pressure from temptation as the desires of our self-centred nature cry out to be met, irrespective of what God has to say about them; and sometimes we face the threat, or even the reality, of persecution. The suffering of the world around us – evidence that the kingdom has not yet come in full – constantly wears us down. And sadly, it's not just a question of turmoil *outside* the Christian community; the painful divisions that exist within the Church take their toll as well.

Although these things may sometimes seem to overwhelm us, they need not. In the midst of sorrow comes joy, and in Holy Communion we have a reminder of the great meal to come. This is a foretaste of the heavenly banquet of the triumphant Messiah, the party in heaven that we shall one day enjoy together in the undiluted presence of the Lord himself. In John's picture of the future in the book of Revelation, an angel describes this event as the 'wedding supper of the Lamb' (Revelation 19:9). Holy Communion reflects the tension between the 'already' and the 'not yet' of our Christian experience. We truly participate in the heavenly banquet – but by faith rather than sight.

This is why, as Paul says, Christians 'proclaim the Lord's death until he comes' (1 Corinthians 11:26). It's something that we do in order to express our confidence in the fact that Jesus will indeed return and take us to be with himself for ever. This meal is, if you like, the first course of the eternal banquet that Christians believe they will enjoy with Jesus and with one another in heaven. That's why it's so appropriate to celebrate and praise him in eager anticipation of the glorious future he has waiting for those who trust in him. Such a focus on what is to come helps to sustain us during times of present pain and difficulty. Part of an early

Christian prayer expresses both this yearning for everything to come right in the end and the confidence that it will: 'As this broken bread was scattered upon the mountains and being gathered together became one, so may your church be gathered together from the ends of the earth into your kingdom; for yours is the glory and the power through Jesus Christ for ever'.[2]

*   *   *

Let all mortal flesh keep silence
and with fear and trembling stand;
set your minds on things eternal,
for with blessing in his hand
Christ our God to earth descending
comes our homage to command.

King of kings, yet born of Mary,
once upon the earth he stood;
Lord of lords we now perceive him
in his body and his blood —
he will give to all the faithful
his own self for heavenly food.

Rank on rank the host of heaven
stream before him on the way;
as the Light of light descending
from the realms of endless day
vanquishes the power of evil,
clears the gloom of hell away.

At his feet the six-winged seraphs,
cherubim with sleepless eye,
veil their faces in his presence
as with ceaseless voice they cry:
Alleluia, alleluia,
alleluia, Lord most high!

(G. Moultrie, 1829–85)[3]

Here and now

However, the New Testament doesn't restrict the coming of the kingdom to the future. With the arrival of Jesus, there's an important sense in which God's kingdom has already arrived. Mark's Gospel records the gist of his message right from the start of his public ministry: '"The time has come," he said. "The kingdom of God is near. Repent and believe the good news!"' (Mark 1:15). What Jesus meant, and what his work of preaching and healing decisively demonstrated, was that God's reign over sin and evil was *already* beginning to come about. The challenge for *all* Jesus' followers in *every* generation is to see God's gracious rule extended in the lives of individuals and in the structures of the world around us. Just as we *receive* a foretaste of the banquet of heaven in Holy Communion so too we're encouraged to *be* a foretaste of the life of heaven to those around us. It's not just a question of waiting for the final denouement at the end of time; there is work to be done here and now.

One aspect of this which has come more to the fore in recent years is in the area of prayer for healing. As we celebrate the living presence of the Lord and focus on his love and compassion, it's only natural that we should bring before him our own need for healing and also the needs of others. In most services, this forms an important part of the prayers of intercession. In addition, some churches include an opportunity for members of the congregation to come forward and receive specific prayer for themselves or those close to them.

> Generous God, we thank you for the *power* of your
>   Holy Spirit.
> We ask that we may be strengthened to serve you better.
> Lord, come to bless us:
> **and fill us with your Spirit.**
>
> We thank you for the *wisdom* of your Holy Spirit.
> We ask you to help us understand better your will for us.

Lord, come to bless us:
and fill us with your Spirit.

We thank you for the *peace* of your Holy Spirit.
We ask you to keep us confident of your love
wherever you call us.
Lord, come to bless us:
and fill us with your Spirit.

We thank you for the *healing* of your Spirit.
We ask you to bring reconciliation and wholeness
where there is division, sickness and sorrow.
Lord, come to bless us:
and fill us with your Spirit.

We thank you for the *gifts* of your Holy Spirit.
We ask you to equip us for the work you have given us.
Lord, come to bless us:
and fill us with your Spirit.

We thank you for the *fruit* of your Holy Spirit.
We ask you to reveal in our lives the love of Jesus.
Lord, come to bless us:
and fill us with your Spirit.

We thank you for the *breath* of your Holy Spirit
given by the risen Lord.
We ask you to keep the whole church, living and departed,
in the joy of eternal life.
Lord, come to bless us:
and fill us with your Spirit.

Generous God, you sent your Holy Spirit
upon your Messiah at the River Jordan,
and upon the disciples in the upper room.
In your mercy fill us with your Spirit:

hear our prayer,
and make us one in heart and mind
to serve you with joy for ever. Amen.[4]

*   *   *

Here is bread, here is wine,
Christ is with us, he is with us.
Break the bread, taste the wine,
Christ is with us here.

In this bread there is healing,
in this cup there's life for ever.
In this moment, by the Spirit,
Christ is with us here.

Here is grace, here is peace,
Christ is with us, he is with us.
Know his grace, find his peace,
feast on Jesus here.

Here we are, joined in one,
Christ is with us, he is with us.
We'll proclaim, till he comes,
Jesus crucified.

(Graham Kendrick)[5]

*   *   *

Joining with heaven

Another aspect of this look forward to the future is the way
that services of Holy Communion often incorporate more than a
hint of the worship of heaven. Here are two occasions where the
Bible allows us to peek through the windows of heaven to witness

its worship. The first, from the Old Testament, comes in the writings of the prophet Isaiah:

> [1]In the year that King Uzziah died, I saw the Lord seated on a throne, high and exalted, and the train of his robe filled the temple. [2]Above him were seraphs, each with six wings: With two wings they covered their faces, with two they covered their feet, and with two they were flying. [3]And they were calling to one another: 'Holy, holy, holy is the LORD Almighty; the whole earth is full of his glory.' [4]At the sound of their voices the doorposts and thresholds shook and the temple was filled with smoke.
>
> (Isaiah 6:1–4)

The same note recurs in the book of Revelation at the end of the New Testament:

> [2]. . . I was in the Spirit, and there before me was a throne in heaven with someone sitting on it. [3]And the one who sat there had the appearance of jasper and carnelian. A rainbow, resembling an emerald, encircled the throne. [4]Surrounding the throne were twenty-four other thrones, and seated on them were twenty-four elders. They were dressed in white and had crowns of gold on their heads. [5]From the throne came flashes of lightning, rumblings and peals of thunder. Before the throne, seven lamps were blazing. These are the seven spirits of God. [6]Also before the throne there was what looked like a sea of glass, clear as crystal. In the centre, around the throne, were four living creatures, and they were covered with eyes, in front and in back. [7]The first living creature was like a lion, the second was like an ox, the third had a face like a man, the fourth was like a flying eagle. [8]Each of the four living creatures had six wings and was covered with eyes all around, even under his wings. Day and night they never stop saying: 'Holy, holy, holy is the Lord God Almighty, who was, and is, and is to come.'

[9]Whenever the living creatures give glory, honour and thanks to him who sits on the throne and who lives for ever and ever, [10]the twenty-four elders fall down before him who sits on the throne, and worship him who lives for ever and ever. They lay their crowns before the throne and say: [11]'You are worthy, our Lord and God, to receive glory and honour and power, for you created all things, and by your will they were created and have their being'.

(Revelation 4:2–11)

Many churches include a conscious echo of these passages in their services of Holy Communion, such as the use of the *Sanctus* (from the Latin for 'holy'). Here, for example, is part of one of the Eucharistic Prayers from the *Alternative Service Book 1980* used by the Church of England: '. . . Therefore with angels and archangels, and with all the company of heaven, we proclaim your great and glorious name, for ever praising you and saying: Holy, holy, holy, Lord, God of power and might, heaven and earth are full of your glory. Hosanna in the highest . . .' A little later in this prayer, this accent on the unity between our worship on earth and the worship of those in heaven is repeated: '. . . with all who stand before you in earth and heaven, we worship you, Father almighty, in songs of everlasting praise . . .'

In this way, we express the fellowship we enjoy, not only with the worshippers we can see around us, but also with those we cannot see – both on earth and in heaven. However few we may be, however feeble our efforts to praise God may seem to be, we are not alone. A well-known hymn, 'Praise, my soul, the King of heaven' expresses this:

Angels, help us to adore Him;
ye behold Him face to face;
sun and moon, bow down before Him;
dwellers all in time and space.
Alleluia! Alleluia!
Praise with us the God of grace.

(H. F. Lyte)

CHAPTER 8

Looking out
Evangelism and Holy Communion

HOLY COMMUNION is a meal for those who belong to Christ – so much so that, in the early days of the Church, the unbaptised would be ushered out of church before the prayers and the exchange of the Peace. This dismissal of non-communicants is one possible explanation of the use of the word 'Mass' (from the Latin word *missa*, meaning 'to dismiss') to describe Holy Communion.

But it can be argued that this was a waste of a good opportunity. It was John Wesley, the founder of Methodism, who described Holy Communion as 'a converting ordinance'. For here is an occasion where people can both hear and see the drama of salvation. They can experience Christ's living presence among his people. They can catch a glimpse of the glory of heaven, as the Church strains to join the angels and archangels in their unending worship of the Lamb of God.

A good example of the evangelistic effectiveness of the Lord's Supper is the conversion of Wesley's own mother, Susanna. In his diary for 3rd September 1739, Wesley records what happened when she heard the minister saying 'the blood of our Lord Jesus Christ, which was given for thee': '. . . the words struck my heart, and I knew God for Christ's sake had forgiven me all my sins'.

Forty years later, a young man named Charles Simeon left Eton School to begin his studies at King's College, Cambridge. During his first week, he received a note from the Provost requiring his attendance at Holy Communion in three weeks' time. It was to be a significant event in his Christian pilgrimage. Years later he described his feeling at the time that 'Satan himself was as fit to attend as I.' In an effort to overcome this sense of unworthiness he found a book by Bishop Thomas Wilson called *A Short and Plain Instruction for the Lord's Supper*. Eventually Charles realised what Jesus Christ had achieved on the cross for him: 'I can transfer all my guilt to Another! I will not bear them on my soul a moment longer.' It was Holy Week, the week before Easter 1779.

> Accordingly I sought to lay my sins upon the sacred head of Jesus; and on the Wednesday began to have a hope of mercy; on the Thursday that hope increased; on the Friday and Saturday it became more strong; and on the Sunday morning, Easter Day, April 4th, I awoke early with those words upon my heart and lips, 'Jesus Christ is risen today! Hallelujah! Hallelujah!' From that hour peace flowed in rich abundance into my soul, and at the Lord's Table in our Chapel I had the sweetest access to God through my blessed Saviour.[1]

Such incidents are not limited to the distant past. At a service of Holy Communion during a Christian event in England called 'Soul Survivor', a whole group of young people were so moved by what the service conveyed of the love of Christ that, there and then, they handed their lives over to God and became Christians.

Evangelism, though, is not the primary goal of Holy Communion. The main aim is to worship the Lord, but authentic worship always has the side-effect of attracting outsiders to the reality of a relationship with the living God. As Jesus himself promised, '. . . I, when I am lifted up from the earth, will draw all men to myself' (John 12:32). Nothing lifts Jesus up more effectively than the proclamation, through word and sacrament, of the cross.

We constantly need the stimulus to look outwards rather than remain turned in on ourselves. Michael Green makes the point well: 'The eucharist is battle rations for Christian warriors, not cream cake for Christian layabouts'.[2] And so, as one of the prayers after Holy Communion in the Church of England's *Alternative Service Book 1980* puts it:

Almighty God,
we thank you for feeding us
with the body and blood of your Son Jesus Christ.
Through him we offer you our souls and bodies
to be a living sacrifice.
Send us out
in the power of your Spirit
to live and work
to your praise and glory. Amen.

*   *   *

Strengthen for service, Lord, the hands
that holy things have taken;
let ears that now have heard your songs
to clamour never waken.

Lord, may the tongues which 'Holy' sang
keep free from all deceiving;
the eyes which saw your love be bright,
the glorious hope perceiving.

The feet that tread your holy courts
from light be never banished;
the bodies by your Body fed,
be with new life replenished.[3]

❧ Further reading

Dare to Break Bread: Eucharist in Desert and City, Geoffrey Howard (Darton, Longman & Todd, 1992).

Prayers of the Eucharist: Early and Reformed, R. C. D. Jasper & G. J. Cuming (Collins, 1975).

The Study of Liturgy, ed: Cheslyn Jones, Geoffrey Wainwright, Edward Yarnold (SPCK, 1978).

The Banquet's Wisdom: A Short History of the Theologies of the Lord's Supper, Gary Macy (Paulist Press, 1992).

Last Supper & Lord's Supper, I. Howard Marshall (Paternoster, 1980).

The Worship of God, Ralph P. Martin (Paternoster, 1982).

Lively Sacrifice: The Eucharist in the Church of England Today, Michael Perham (SPCK, 1992).

The Cross of Christ, John Stott (IVP, 1985), especially chapter 10.

I Believe in The Church, David Watson (Hodder & Stoughton, 1978), chapter 14.

❧ Notes

Foreword

1. *John Wesley 1703–1791: A Bicentennial Tribute* by John Walsh. Friends of Dr Williams's Library, 14 Gordon Square, London WC1H 0AG, 1993.

Chapter 1

1. From section 67.1 of Justin Martyr, *The First Apology*, as quoted in *Prayers of the Eucharist: Early and Reformed* by R. C. D. Jasper and G. J. Cuming (Collins, 1975).

Chapter 2

1. As quoted by Peter G. Cobb in *The Study of Liturgy*, ed. Cheslyn Jones, Geoffrey Wainwright and Edward Yarnold (SPCK, 1978).

2. By Horatius Bonar (1808–89), as revised by Jubilate Hymns. © Jubilate Hymns; used by kind permission.

Chapter 3

1. From *The Lord's Supper* by William Barclay (SCM Press, 1967).

2. Copyright © 1991 Make Way Music, P.O. Box 263, Croydon, Surrey CR9 5AP. All rights reserved. International copyright secured. Used by permission.

3. From the Scottish Liturgy 1992, © Scottish Episcopal Church.

4. In Book 1, Chapter 12, of *A Defence of the True and Catholic Doctrine of the Sacrament of the Body and Blood of our Saviour Jesus Christ*.

Chapter 4

1. From *The Edge of Glory: Prayers in the Celtic Tradition* by David Adam (Triangle/SPCK, 1985).

2. e.g. Scripture Union (Queensway House, 207-9 Queensway, Bletchley, Bucks MK2 2EB, tel: 01908 856000) or The Bible Reading Fellowship (Peter's Way, Sandy Lane West, Oxford OX4 5HG, tel: 01865 748227).

3. Published by Hodder & Stoughton in 1981.

Chapter 5

1. *The Message of John*, Bruce Milne (IVP, 1993), p. 113.

2. By J. Conder; in this version, © Jubilate Hymns; used by kind permission.

3. e.g. the publication of *Patterns for Worship* (Church House Publishing, 1995), a resource book that has been officially commended for use in the Church of England.

4. The original version of this hymn was written by Frances Ridley Havergal (1836–79). This version is © Jubilate Hymns; used by kind permission.

5. © Oxford University Press; reprinted by permission.

6. An example of this appears in the writings of Justin Martyr: 'We do not receive these things as common bread or common drink; but just as our Saviour Jesus Christ, being incarnate through the word of God, took flesh and blood for our salvation, so too we have been taught that the food over which thanks has been given by the prayer of the Word who is from him, from which

our flesh and blood are fed by transformation, is both the flesh and blood of that incarnate Jesus' (*First Apology*, 66.1)

7. From *Your Confirmation: A Christian Handbook for Adults* by John Stott (Hodder & Stoughton, 1991).

8. Copyright © 1985 Kingsway's Thankyou Music, P.O. Box 75, Eastbourne, Sussex BN23 6NW. Used by permission.

9. ARCIC's *Agreed Statement on Eucharistic Doctrine*, 1971, 11.5.

10. This early Christian hymn dates from at least the end of the fourth century and is now used by many churches in their services of Holy Communion. The version set out here is from the Church of England's *Book of Common Prayer*.

11. After J. Franck (1618–77) by Catherine Winkworth (1827–78); in this version © Jubilate Hymns; used by kind permission.

Chapter 6

1. From *Dare to Break Bread: Eucharist in Desert and City* by Geoffrey Howard (Darton, Longman & Todd, 1992).

2. © 1971, 1995 Stainer & Bell Ltd for the world except USA, Canada, Australia and New Zealand. Reprinted by permission.

Chapter 7

1. © Christopher Porteous, © Jubilate Hymns; used by kind permission.

2. From section 9 of an early Christian manual on morals and church practice known as *The Didache* (from the Greek for 'teaching').

3. A hymn by G. Moultrie (1829–85) based on *The Liturgy of St James*. This version is © Jubilate Hymns; used by kind permission.

4. This responsive intercession from Patterns of Worship (Church House Publishing, 1995) is copyright © the PCC, Holy Trinity, Guildford; used by kind permission.

5. Copyright © 1991 Make Way Music, P.O. Box 263, Croydon, Surrey CR9 5AP. All rights reserved. International copyright secured. Used by permission.

Chapter 8

1. Quoted by Hugh Evan Hopkin in *Charles Simeon of Cambridge* (Hodder & Stoughton, 1977), p. 28.

2. *To Corinth with Love* by Michael Green (Hodder & Stoughton, 1982), p. 49.

3. From a fifth-century Syriac liturgy. Tr. C. W. Humphreys (1841–1921) and Percy Dearmer (1867–1936) (altd.), © Oxford University Press; reprinted by permission.